Makram El Kadi
and Ziad Jamaleddine

Tom Coward
Daisy Froud
Vincent Lacovara
and Geoff Shearcroft

Hernán Díaz Alonso

Renewing Architectural Typologies

Yale School of Architecture
180 York Street
New Haven, Connecticut 06520
www.architecture.yale.edu

Distributed by
ActarD
151 Grand Street, 5th Floor
New York, New York 10013
www.actar-d.com

This book was made possible through an endowment for the Louis I. Kahn Visiting Assistant Professorship at the Yale School of Architecture. It is the fifth in a series of publications of the Louis I. Kahn Assistant Professorship published through the dean's office.

Editors: Nina Rappaport and Letícia Wouk Almino
Design: MGMT. design

Library of Congress data: available upon request.

ISBN 978-0-9893317-5-3 (pbk.)

Louis I. Kahn Visiting Assistant Professorship

The Louis I. Kahn Visiting Assistant Professorship is Yale's second endowed chair to honor the architect. It was established in 2004 to bring to the school younger architects who practice and teach, offering them the opportunity to lead advanced design studios and seminars. The Kahn Visiting Assistant Professorship carries with it the expectation that the work of the visiting professors and their students will be published so that others may benefit from the ideas developed and exchanged in the studios.

Louis I. Kahn (1901–1974), perhaps the greatest American architect of the post-World War II era, was closely associated with Yale as a teacher and practicing architect. Yale is home to his first important building, the extension to the Art Gallery (1951–53), and his last, the Center for British Art (1969–77). Kahn was fresh to teaching when he came to Yale in 1947 to begin what would be ten years as chief critic in the architecture school. As a teacher, he worked closely with students encouraging them to go beyond their initial ideas about architecture, as he himself was trying to go beyond his own ideas. Kahn inspired a generation of architects, leading them to new insights that became the basis of their independent work.

Twenty-one studios have been offered by Louis I. Kahn Visiting Assistant Professors, beginning with Gregg Pasquarelli, whose studio — along with that of successor appointees, Galia Solomonoff and Mario Gooden — was published in the book *Layered Urbanisms*, in 2007. The studios of the next three appointees to the chair, Jeanne Gang, Sunil Bald, and Mark Tsurumaki, were documented in *Negotiated Terrains*, in 2009. The studio led by FAT Architects — Sean Griffiths, Sam Jacob, and Charles Holland — collaborating with Edward P. Bass Visiting Fellow developer Nick Johnson of Urban Splash — was published in *Urban Integration / Bishopsgate Goods Yard*, in 2010. The studios of Christopher Sharples, William Sharples, and Ali Rahim were published in the volume, *Turbulence*, in 2011. *Architecture Inserted*, published in 2012, presented the work and studios of Eric Bunge and Mimi Hoang, Chris Perry, and Liza Fior with Katherine Clarke.

This volume, *Renewing Architectural Typologies: Mosque, Archive, House*, documenting the studios of Makram El Kadi and Ziad Jamaleddine of L.E.FT Architects, Tom Coward, Daisy Froud, Vincent Lacovara, and Geoff Shearcroft, of AOC, and Hernán Díaz Alonso of Xefirotarch, reflects, as do its predecessors, Yale's studio pedagogy which is founded on the bedrock of diversity and independent thinking.

Foreword

Renewing Architectural Typologies: Mosque, Archive, House, documents three advanced studios of the Louis I. Kahn Visiting Assistant Professorship, where emerging teacher-practitioners are invited to offer an advanced studio and a seminar at the school: Makram El Kadi with Ziad Jamaleddine of the New York and Beirut-based practice L.E.FT, who as the fifteenth Louis I. Kahn Visiting Assistant Professors offered the studio, The Expanded Mosque, Spring 2011. El Kadi attended the American University of Beirut and then received his Masters of Architecture at Parsons School of Design. Earlier in his career he worked for Steven Holl Architects, with whom he is now working on the Beirut Marina Project, along with his partner Jamaleddine, who attended the Harvard GSD. The firm received the 2002 Young Architects Award from the Architectural League of New York and in 2010 the League selected it as part of its Emerging Voices program. The firm was also a 2010 Finalist for the Design Vanguard of *Architectural Record* magazine.

Tom Coward, Daisy Froud, Vincent Lacovara, and Geoff Shearcroft, of the London-based practice AOC, were the sixteenth Louis I. Kahn Visiting Assistant Professors and led the studio, Synthesizing a Participative Architecture, in Fall 2011. The firm founded in 2003 consists of three architects, who all attended the Royal College of Art with Froud, who attended Cambridge University, and is a collaborative planner. The work of AOC has been exhibited at the Venice Architecture Biennale in 2008 and they each teach at universities in England.

The fourteenth Kahn Visiting Assistant Professor, Hernán Díaz Alonso of Los Angeles-based Xefirotarch, led the studio Type Versus Species in Fall 2010. After considering a career in film making, Alonso attended the National University of Rosario Argentina and then Columbia School of Architecture after which he worked for Miralles Tagliabue EMBT Architects in Barcelona, and Peter Eisenman in New York. Alonso's L.A.-based practice Xefirotarch, which he founded in 2001, designs installations and architectural works. His essays have appeared in *AD* and *A+U*, among other journals. His work has been exhibited at SFMoMA and the Art Institute of Chicago and he was the winner of the PS1 MoMA Young Architects program in New York in 2005. Alonso currently teaches at Sci-Arc in Los Angeles.

I would like to acknowledge the collaboration of the Kahn Visiting Assistant Professors and their students in helping to make this book possible. Recognition is also due to the editorial team of Nina Rappaport (Publications Director) and Letícia Wouk Almino (M.Arch '11). This book makes a strong case for rigorous studio education based in creative analysis of program that allows the design process to expand from typically diagrammatic solutions into a dynamic architectural discourse focused on form.

Robert A.M. Stern
Dean and J.M. Hoppin Professor

Introduction

Renewing Architectural Typologies: House, Mosque, Archive is the fifth book to feature the work of the Louis I. Kahn Visiting Assistant Professorship and the work of the advanced studios at the Yale School of Architecture.

This book includes research and designs that emerged from studios taught at Yale by Makram El Kadi with Ziad Jamaleddine of New York and Beirut-based architectural practice L.E.FT; Tom Coward, Daisy Froud, Vincent Lacovara, and Geoff Shearcroft, of the London-based practice AOC; and Hernán Díaz Alonso of Los Angeles-based Xefirotarch. By challenging established architectural typologies, the projects explore how the cultural identity of traditional and known building types may be synthesized with new programs in order to better address the changing needs of the twenty-first century public.

Makram El Kadi and Ziad Jamaleddine question the established typology of the mosque as a way of proposing new possibilities for the future. Following extensive research into the complex liturgical and communal functions of the mosque, the studio attempts to understand how the architecture of the mosque can foster dialogue with other programs, religious or secular, and thus negotiate the different facets of Islamic society.

Tom Coward, Daisy Froud, Vincent Lacovara, and Geoff Shearcroft examine how the old public museums of London may be informed by the "big box" typology to produce an architecture that presents new ways of viewing and understanding artifacts. By subverting preconceived notions of the past, the studio produces designs that reconceptualize the institution and its relationship between visitor, artifact, and place.

Hernán Díaz Alonso explores the idea of home by subverting the typology of the house, and thus presenting radical possibilities of inhabitation. The house occupies a site in Los Angeles, the birthplace of California Modernism, and is subject to transformation through a sequence of three acts that employs a cellular spatial logic. The student projects address the basic idea of home, while also endeavoring to replace the typical house type with a new definition of species.

Each section of the book begins with an interview with the architects about the work of their firm. The essays framing the studio explorations introduce the studio research and design strategies, providing insight into the pedagogical approach of these practitioner-educators and proposing ways to address the changing needs of our technologically driven global society while maintaining a dialogue with the past.

The editors would like to thank the professors and the students for helping to make this document possible. From El Kadi and Jamaleddine's studio, we would like to thank Melissa Bauld, Hillary Bingnear, Amy Chang, Jacob Dugopolski, Erin Dwyer, Anne Mason Kemper, Ronald Lim, SeoYoung Shin, David Tasman, and Letícia Wouk Almino. From the AOC studio, we would like to thank John Taylor Bachman, Christos Bolos, Vincent Calabro, Stephen Gage, Francesco Galetto, Erik Hermann, Lane Rick, and Ian Starling. From the Alonso studio, the editors would like to thank Patrick Delahoy, Yang Guang, Jin Kim, Gary Ku, Liam Lowry, Emer O'Daly, Andrew Smith-Rasmussen, Kyle Stover, and Hoey Yip. Special recognition is due to Kyle Stover for his editorial work on the Alonso studio section.

We extend our utmost appreciation to Sarah Gephart of MGMT. design, copy editor David Delp, and Dean Robert A.M. Stern. We hope this volume presents new possibilities for architectural exploration and elicits debate on the future of design.

Nina Rappaport and Letícia Wouk Almino
Editors

L.E.FT

The Expanded Mosque

L.E.FT with Steven Holl Architects, Beirut Marina, Beirut, Lebanon, 2013.

Makram El Kadi with his partner Ziad Jamaleddine founded the Beirut and New York-based architecture firm L.E.FT. They were the Louis I. Kahn Visiting Professors in Spring 2011 teaching an advanced studio at Yale. Below is a discussion with Nina Rappaport about their practice and teaching.

Nina Rappaport: As new architectural practices become global, it is commonplace to see well-educated, foreign architects coming to the United States or Europe for graduate studies and staying, while retaining close ties to their home country, especially when there is a politically or economically difficult situation. How have you been able to practice effectively in both Beirut and New York City? Makram El Kadi: The fact that both my partner, Ziad Jamaleddine, and I studied as undergraduates at the American University of Beirut created a tie for us with the States. We were exposed to contemporary architectural thinking in the United States through our American teachers. So we wanted to continue this relationship by having our office based in New York City and looking at our home country through the quasi-objective lens that distance gives us. Europe has closer ties to Lebanon through its past French colonial presence, but we saw the States as an added layer that we needed to understand.

How does your background affect your architectural practice? Do you think of yourselves as global architects? We consider ourselves global, but you cannot go beyond your own identity and upbringing. In that sense we try to put ourselves outside of a specific identity, and we try not to work with the normative identity politics. We do consider ourselves contextual, not in the normative sense of the word but in relation to how we position architecture within a specific stylistic context. We try to look at context within a sociopolitical definition.

How did growing up with the reality of war and fractured political divisions influence your practice? We experienced all aspects of the war. We went to shelters; we didn't have a normal childhood in the traditional sense. But we don't regret it at all, because it was a very informative experience. When we later studied the work of Foucault, we really understood what he meant when he said that politics is a continuation of war by other means. That is how we perceive the contemporary world: as a continuous state of war that doesn't necessarily involve military action but is a series of negotiations in which architecture has a role to play.

How is architecture a negotiator in spatial politics? We understand architectural production as occurring in a place in which space is air imbued with politics. It's not a formalist or aesthetic understanding of architecture. We don't dismiss it per se; on the contrary, we push our formal agenda in a way that promotes innovation. But we try to understand architecture operationally, not necessarily from the new interest in sustainability that everybody has, for example, but through another filter or lens.

It is one thing to say that architecture and space are political or influenced by politics, but is a building actually understood as political by the people who experience it? To some degree, we try to put the user — this is going to sound negative, but it's not — in an uncomfortable position vis-à-vis his or her experience and/or presence in the space, as well as their preconceived ideas about space and context in general.

The unexpected experience that makes someone think twice about their surroundings takes some wit. How have you expressed this at a small scale? For example, we once began an apartment interior project with the placement of the toilet-paper roll. We placed it at the edge, between the very private space of the bathroom and the living room, putting different issues at the forefront that are usually on the back burner.

What is the public value in these speculative provocations? Are you making the public feel that same kind of awkwardness you effected by putting the toilet paper in the door? How does this idea of awkwardness in a building transfer to an active project as an agency of change? Although they are considered utopian projects, they serve as critiques since they showcase inherent prejudices. The more they provoke, the more successful they are. The uneasiness has practical aspects. Our project, Offshore Urbanism, triggered a debate about the need for a national shelter in Lebanon and for public coastal transportation after the 2006 bombing of Lebanese highways by the Israelis. The by-product was the water-taxi concept developed by some students.

Are you taking a risk by doing this? In the Middle East, either you segregate yourself from the debates that are happening or you integrate and take a side. We're trying to instigate. It's a third option.

How did your work with Steven Holl bring you back to Beirut after graduate school? We asked him to participate in a competition for a student center at the American University of Beirut. Although he didn't win, Solidere [the construction company rebuilding the downtown] asked him to work on a project for the Beirut marina. So, this led to us getting the commission for the temporary Beirut Exhibition Center.

Aside from the façade and reflectivity, what were the site and urban concepts that connected to the city and the people there? We worked from a master plan with the building, which had a sculpture garden and a garden café on the south end to activate that part of the city. The interior comprises a series of movable partitions that accommodate the different exhibitions. In the design of the Beirut Cultural Center, we are doing the same thing. We are not proposing a precise architecture; we're taking the landscape as a blank canvas and transforming it into a mountain; with a roofscape formed by insertions of typical vernacular balconies that are closed off as private spaces.

What project did you focus on in your Yale studio? The studio is called "The Expanded Mosque." In contemporary political discourse, Islam is under a magnifying glass. In contrast to both Judaism and Christianity in the Middle East, Islam is the fastest-growing religion, and by 2025 it will be the biggest on earth. We wanted to critique, architecturally, both an imported Modernism that is dissociated from contextual considerations and a reconstruction of the present in the image of an idealized past. So there are two extremes. Within the mosque project there is a broader program beyond the mosque's liturgical function as a community gathering place. Through this loophole in the typology, we looked at how the physical space of the mosque and social space of Islam can have a dialogue with other programs. It is an uncomfortable situation. It is like the way Bucky Fuller defines architecture in terms of its weight. We're trying to do the same thing but on a more political level — viewing architecture beyond proportion and style.

Have you been able to build a project at a larger scale that successfully negotiates the spectrum between the political and the personal? How do your buildings actually connect the architectural details to the larger realm of the city and its political issues? For the recently completed Beirut Exhibition Center, we made a custom skin out of corrugated anodized aluminum that creates a mirror to reflect a city that will be in the process of developing for the next twenty years. The urban center was empty during the civil war, and our project was the first in this bare landscape. It is a placeholder, in a way.

You have been investigating these issues in a series of projects that are speculative, provocative, and that push the comfort zone politically. How have you taken risks with these, and what have they accomplished beyond the competition phase? The first was the 2006 Martyrs' Square competition for a site called the Green Line, a void where the 2005 demonstrations occured and that during the civil war divided predominantly Christian East Beirut from predominantly Muslim West Beirut. It is a fault line, and many architects would try to rebuild it as a tie to try to go beyond the wounds of the past and erase what happened, in an amnesiac sense, to be able to move forward. But the end of the Lebanese civil war was not achieved by reconciliation; it was an international de facto decision made on behalf of the population. Lebanon didn't resolve many of the issues that caused the war, so to come and erase a big chunk of our history is problematic. Instead, we have kept it as a separation line by turning it into a demarcation between two sports teams, taking it away from the militants.

How have these speculative projects been received in Beirut? And how are they both based in reality but also beyond the norm of policies that have developed? Usually, not so well. The second project was Offshore Urbanism, based on the 1930s radio station Radio Luxembourg, which tried to bypass the monopoly of the BBC on commercial shortwave radio by relocating from London to Luxembourg to circumvent local laws. We have an idea that future conflicts between Lebanon and Israel need a massive evacuation plan for the Lebanese population — through a series of barges along the coastline. The minute they reach international waters, they could address social issues that are not considered legal on shore, like civil marriage. Through the lens

L.E.FT, Beirut Exhibition Center, Beirut, Lebanon, 2011.

L.E.FT, Qortuba Clubhouse, Tennis Court View, Qortuba, Kuwait, 2013.

of this continuous war between Lebanon and Israel, we are trying to go beyond the immediate politics of it, to be "political" not in the more yellow-journalism sense of the word but by looking at taboos in society that are put on hold because of the bigger problem of external politics. The intention of the mosque studio was to create a dialogue between the religious and the secular. We question this stagnating typology and try to project new possibilities for the future.

To make it more contemporary? To make it more contemporary but not necessarily more modern. There is a misconception that Islam is not modern. In Islam, there are the seeds of modernity that led to the Western Enlightenment project. So we're going to unravel this concept in the studio for a new mosque in the city of Tripoli linked to an international fair, designed in 1963 by Oscar Niemeyer. The mosque would provide foot traffic to the fair, and the fair would inflict its program onto the mosque.

You are not afraid to address sensitive social issues in these politically contested sites. Of course we have a solution for the Middle East. [*Laughter*]

Yet you also make aesthetic projects with a formal focus on materials. How do you combine your interest in designing beautiful objects with your interest in addressing complex social-urban issues? Often, the political comes to us from a certain formal experimentation or investigation. We make charts for projects that are typologically, programmatically, or functionally driven by politics. But it's definitely not linear, and we admit that a big part of the process is always intuitive by nature. On the other hand, we read all the newspapers coming out of the Middle East, and when we see something that has spatial ramifications we try to incorporate it into a project.

Have you ever gotten into trouble over there? Lebanon now is divided into two camps, and we find ourselves at odds with both camps, in a way. This is a problem with Lebanon and the Arab world, in general, and is mainly a result of Western intervention, which happened after the onset of the Soviet Union. Both the United States and the Arab monarchies undermined any leftist movement in the Arab world in the battle against Communism. That gap was filled by the Islamists. So our project is to bring to architecture the issues that were at the forefront of the leftist movement.

So that's the story behind your name? Yeah, kind of. But our name is also an acronym. Our first office was a storefront on the Lower East Side, in New York City. So, the name is Lower East Front. But "lower east" and "front" are also directional and spatial in nature.

What are your next provocations that are physically challenging and politically difficult for projects in Lebanon? We are trying to break the geographic ghettoization in different religions. There are the geographies of fear, as social scientists call it, meaning everybody claims their own geography. We are also trying to do as much work as possible in diverse religious settings. We are now doing a pro bono project, a soccer field with amenities, in one of the poorest neighborhoods in southern Lebanon. It is a resistance project at the scale we can offer.

How has your office expanded in the past few years? We just opened a satellite office in Beirut, and I am spending my time getting it up and running. It will cater mostly to construction administration. We do the design in New York, and the back-of-house coordination with the clients and supervision will happen in Beirut. It will be a base for the Middle East projects in Dubai and Saudi Arabia, where we are doing a big residential compound with a clubhouse at its epicenter. In Dubai, we won a competition for a campus. It has a housing component, office spaces, residential spaces, and a mosque. In Lebanon, we are doing six private residences.

What is the direction of your new design work? It's been mostly an investigation into domesticity. We are doing a house for a high profile politician. For that house, specifically, the question is how to mitigate the public persona of the client versus the private nature of the house within the same space. It's a two-story house, so we're creating a horizontal separation between a public space below and a private space on top, which we are intersecting with vertical components that are more ambiguous in that they marry both the public and the private. For another house that we are doing in the mountains, we are continuing earlier investigations of understanding the house as a continuous loop of circulation that travels outside the house without necessarily entering it. It is currently under construction. We're also doing a chicken coop, which would be the first step in what will eventually be a domestic zoo. It's for a family that has a series of different animals, and we are going to do "houses" for the different species.

I am also doing a renovation of an old silk factory outside of Beirut. It's one of the five remaining old silk factories in Lebanon. We are gut renovating it and including a vertical element — a spiral staircase — and an elevator that goes inside the bathroom. The bathroom has a two-way mirror. We are getting bigger and bigger projects but still trying to engage with the smaller scale. At the bigger scale, it is always easier to fall into typological investigations, but, with the small scale, we are able to confront identity politics. We are also doing a lobby renovation for an apartment. Instead of a peephole for the door, we are working with a media artist and making a projection, like a small TV, wherein the eye of the owner would be blinking.

How do you obtain these commissions — through friends and family? There are more Lebanese living outside of Lebanon than inside of Lebanon — the outreach is much bigger than the geographic limits. So, there are many connections, but the job with the Lebanese politician came about because he loved our exhibition center in Beirut. The political scene is divided between those who are pro-West and those who are pro-Iran, and I am doing work for both. It's an interesting balance.

Is it easy to go back and forth between cultures? We believe in contextual specificity, but, at the same time, a bedroom here in the U.S. is the same as a bedroom in Lebanon. There are some differences in the kitchen, though. In the U.S., we love open kitchens, but, in Lebanon, you have to have a secure kitchen in upper class households because you have a maid cooking for you.

The Expanded Mosque

“The contention is that architects, more efficiently than intellectuals and scholars, can resist the devastating violence generated by the confrontation of religion, state, and society (*din*, *dunya*, *dawla* — the three major concepts developed in classical Arabic thought) at a greater scale than all societies and cultures in history have achieved thus far. This means that all important architectural achievements contribute either to strengthening the dominant ideology in any given historical tradition and political order, or to creating a breakthrough in the inherited, imposed system of values and beliefs.”

Mohammed Arkoun (*Islamic Culture, Modernity, Architecture*, 1986)

One of the fastest-growing religions today, Islam is expected to be the biggest religion by 2025. With its 1.2 billion followers only second to Christianity, it includes nineteen to twenty-two percent of the world's population. Contrary to a top-heavy Christianity (ratio of elderly to young population is high), Islam is bottom-heavy and grows at an estimated 2.9 percent annually. Yet when it comes to its architectural representation, the mosque, a paradox manifests itself: though more frequented than churches, the mosque is far less subject to architectural experimentation than the church. Parallel to the symposium "Middle Ground/Middle East" on religious architecture in the Middle East held at Yale, the studio addressed the archetype of the mosque in a new hybrid understanding of its program, one that redefines it beyond its current restrictions to liturgical functions. In the process, the studio studied the relation between the physical space of the mosque and the social space of Islam.

Given the lack of specific typology, the mosque can mitigate between social and religious functions. From the two possible translations of the word *mosque* into Arabic, *jamee* or *masjid*, a difference was emphasized between the mosque as a community center/prayer space (*jamee* means "place of gathering" in Arabic) and the mosque as a purely praying facility (*masjid* means "place of prostration" in Arabic). The students were asked to think of programs that could be added to the function of the Mosque and form its expanded physical and programmatic nature. In this sense, the studio addressed the archetype of the mosque in a new hybrid understanding of its program, one that redefines it beyond its current restrictions to liturgical functions and, instead, into both the cultural and the social spaces.

No specific archetype exists for the mosque. One of the first mosques, that of the Prophet Mohammad in Medina (KSA) in the early seventh century, is assumed to have been a simple rectangular structure, with a palm tree as shade for the worshippers, who prayed in parallel lines. Though domes and minarets are typological elements that make mosques identifiable, they are not stylistically inherent to the archetype, though being symbolic in nature, they were not derived from a specific text in the Koran* or the Hadith* (see glossary page 24) but were rather social constructs. The studio began with a study of the development of the different typologies

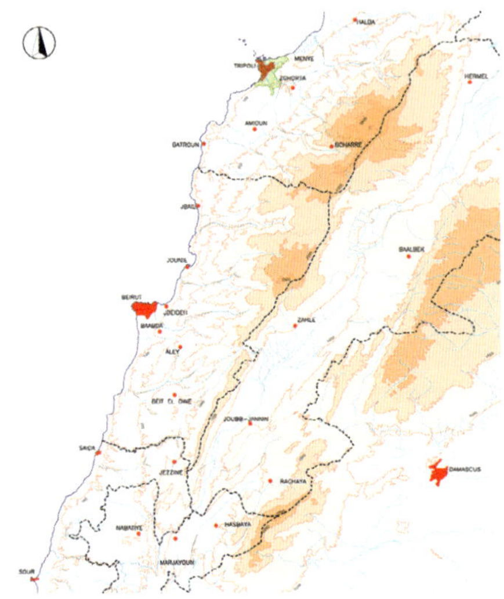

Map of Lebanon.

and the different definitions and categorizations of the mosque, placing them historically in relation to contemporary discourse on Islam. The work of three theoreticians of Islam was posited to the students as a starting point, Mohammed Arkoun, Nasr Hamid Abu Zayd, and Mohammed Abed al Jabri who rejected the current polarization of Arab and Islamic thought between an imported Modernism that disregards Arab tradition and a fundamentalism that would reconstruct the present in the image of an idealized past.

The apparent dichotomy between Islam and Modernity needs a revision. For one, Islam, at its onset, was the forbearer of many Modernist ideas and concepts that preceded and influenced the Enlightenment project. If the product of the Enlightenment was the separation of church and state, in Islam this notion is more complex. On the one hand, the notion of the state didn't exist at the onset of the religion, and it can be argued that the state is more of a Western concept. Was the separation of church and state possible because the Bible was a text in the sense of a narrative compiled from different accounts, and is it less possible in Islam because the Koran as a "revelation" is a meta-narrative?

The first verse of the Koran stipulates a reading: "Read (with the name of Allah)." The word *Koran* itself is a derivative of "reading".

However, Islam with its genesis as a revelation (*mounzal*) is conceived as a narrative that has the seeds of being textual through the notion of *ijtihad* — or opinions in jurisprudence, as opposed to *taqlid* or imitation of the text, which makes the text overdetermined in the Foucauldian sense of deference or, in French, *dif-*

Oscar Niemeyer, Heliport, International Fair of Tripoli, Tripoli, Lebanon, 1975.

ference. If this is the case and Islam can be perceived as a text, one can wonder if we are heading toward a separation of church and state in Islam as well, and if a secularization of Islam can be achieved by practicing the Koran as a text. This is where the notion of *din*, *dunya*, and *dawla* (or religion, society, and state) is relevant in its breaking of the dialectic between Western notions of church and state. To this effect, *dunya* as a concept seems to offer contiguity between the mosque and the state that might preclude the need for a separation between both. This notion also shows that, through this continuity, Islam is inherently political and cannot but be. Its militarization is the problematic exaggeration of its political condition, not its political predisposition.

As architects, we can stipulate on the possible architectural implications of the physical space of the mosque in relationship to the social space of Islam, within this notion of continuity between state/society/mosque. Historically, the mosque offered programmatic hybridity beyond its religious functions (be it schools or hammams, and so on) in comparison to the church, which sat secluded in its own public square. It is potentially through this expanded notion of the program — going beyond the liturgical — that architects can reflect on the notion of the interplay between *din*, *dunya*, and *dawla* to find the space of negotiation, of equilibrium, and of critique.

In the case of the mosque, the hybrid nature of its program, which is a hybridity avant la lettre that preceded that in contemporary architectural discourse, can potentially expand this role of social and cultural glue that would link the different components of society beyond a specific religious background, hence becoming this overdetermined text.

It is this programmatic and architectural loophole, similar to the jurisprudence loophole of *ijtihad* in theology, mentioned previously that has the ability to link the mosque to modernity not just stylistically but operationally.

Mosques have always been a reflection of the political condition within which they were built. A quick survey of mosque architecture on the contemporary Arab Middle East landscape reveals a surge in modern mosques typologies in the 1960s and 1970s, with both Arab and Western architects competing to provide daring new directions to mosque design by engaging typologies that addressed the dichotomy

Oscar Niemeyer, Experimental Theater, International Fair of Tripoli, Tripoli, Lebanon, 1975.

between modernity and tradition, while more contemporary examples revert back to neo-classical interpretations of past experimentations. This can be clearly understood if we parallel the architectural history with that of the political scene, in which the heyday of architectural modernity coincided with that of the "pan-Arab" political movements led by Jamal Abdel Nasser. Similarly, the current turmoil in the political landscape, with the rise in conservative religious movements, is reflected as well in a more traditional and conservative approach to architecture.

Within the current Arab Spring that is still developing in several Arab countries in the Middle East, the mosque has proved to be a critical space of dissent. Every Friday, several demonstrations start from neighborhood mosques and move out into the city. The mosque is thus playing the role of the epicenter for the different social movements, and, for the foreseeable future, it will still be the center of social and political life in the Arab world. The challenge is to investigate formal and typological approaches to alleviate the mosque from a purely sacred space to a more modern space, a space where criticality is achieved.

SITE

The site of the proposed mosque was chosen to be a part of Tripoli's Permanent International Fair, designed by Brazilian architect Oscar Niemeyer. Located in the northern part of the country, along the border with Syria, and a two-hour drive from Beirut, Tripoli is Lebanon's second-largest city and port and home to an increasing Muslim population. Estimated at around 500,000 inhabitants, the city went through different historical layers, from the Phoenicians to the Romans to the Mamluks and the Ottoman Empire. It is home to many historical mosques, including the Mamluk Grand Mosque.

The fair itself, designed in 1962 and partially completed in 1974, was never occupied due to the outbreak of the civil war. Situated in an unfinished portion of Niemeyer's master plan, the mosque is positioned along a major coastal highway connecting Lebanon to Syria and forms the entry to the city. The mosque and the fair would develop an osmotic relationship in which the mosque would provide foot traffic to the fair, and the fair, programmed with a larger understanding of its role both regionally and nationally, would provide

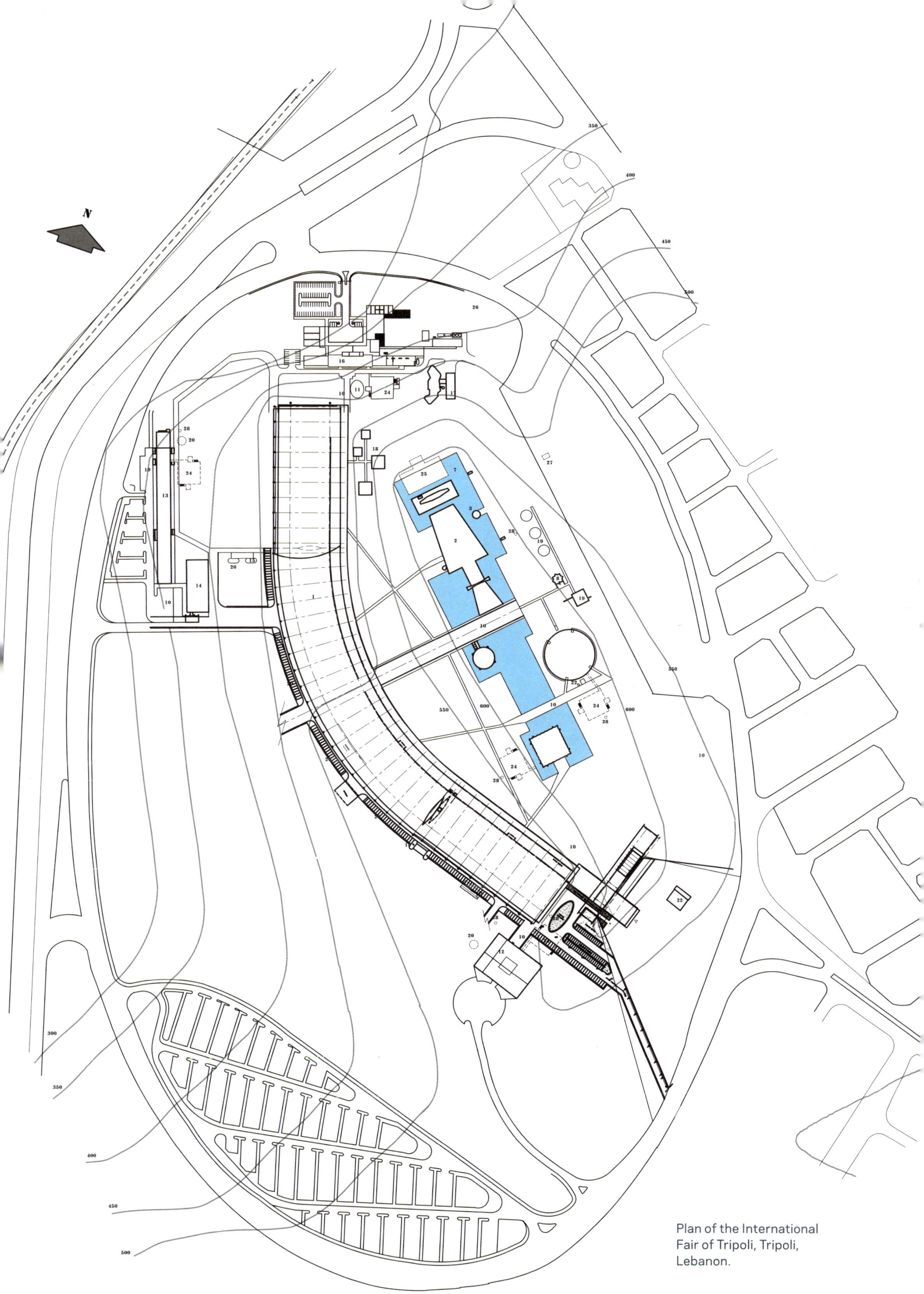

Plan of the International Fair of Tripoli, Tripoli, Lebanon.

Aerial View of Tripoli, Lebanon.

Oscar Niemeyer, Interior View of the Experimental Theater, International Fair of Tripoli, Tripoli, Lebanon, 1975.

the mosque with an extension of its program to the outside life of the city.

METHODOLOGY

Of the several approaches and challenges presented in the studio, three main methodologies — the urban, the programmatic, and the immaterial — informed, to varying degrees, most student projects.

1 Starting with a notion of the overdetermined nature of the mosque's role, at an urban scale was critical. Several approaches were discussed to link the architectural object to the life of the city, either symbolically or physically.

2 Programmatically, the hybrid nature of a mosque with an external function had, on one hand, a more socially conscious approach to the architecture of the mosque and, on the other hand, a banalization of the "sacred" nature of the project into an integration with the "everyday" and the "mundane," rendering the religious more accessible.

3 Finally, most projects incorporated a more immaterial dimension to the project through a study of light at different times of the day and different prayer times, rendering a certain ephemeral quality to the spaces they designed that related back to the programmatic use of the space. Another aspect of this immaterial dimension was the use of water as a design element, mainly through the ablution spaces that were

foregrounded in some cases, and forwarded as main elements of the projects.

The studio started with a research phase in which the students investigated the history and the evolution of the architecture of the mosque, both formally and typologically, from the early days of Islam to contemporary examples of mosque architecture. The different phases of the mosque's development were identified, highlighting the transformative key moments in the development of the typology that go against the received notions of a mosque as having hierarchical components. The next investigation was to look at the taxonomy of the spatial qualities inherent in the mosque design extracted from the previously assigned reading. This exercise allowed the students to form a better understanding of each system and typology in relation to their historical and geographical contexts. The students were then asked to isolate one major element of the mosque typology (minaret, dome, hypostyle hall/courtyard, ablution space, *qibla* wall) and formulate a building proposition that would have that element as the dominant form, with the other elements derived from it, yet still fulfill the functions of a mosque. Students then developed an option for each element as well as iterations within each option based on one or more formal manipulations (scaling, rotating, subtracting, multiplication). The intent was to see the limits of breaking the historical typology of the mosque into each of its elements to reconstruct it in light of a new understanding of that typology.

GLOSSARY

Qur'an: in Arabic means "recitation." The "five pillars" of fundamental observances are:

1 The acceptance of the shahada: "There is no God but the God and Muhammad is his Messenger."
2 Prayer, or namaz, is to be performed five times per day (at dawn, around midday, afternoon, sunset, night before going to bed).
3 Alms, or zakat.
4 Fasting: Ramadan is observed during the ninth lunar month of the Muslim year.
5 Pilgrimage, or haj, to Mecca.

Hadith: the "traditions" or "sayings" relating to the life of Muhammad. There are two kinds of revelation: that which is recited - the Qur'an; and that which is read but not recited - hadith.
Sharia: the legal system in keeping with the code of behavior called for by the Qur'an and the hadith. Original meaning in Arabic "path leading to the water," meaning the "way to the source of life."
Sunna: the guiding principal for correct behavior and belief was respect for tradition. In ancient Arabic meant "ancestral precedent" or the "custom of the tribe." The practice and precept of the Prophet as transmitted by the hadith. Those who accept this principle are called Sunnis, and account for eighty-five percent of all Muslims.
Ablution: typically linked to a source of running water but in some regions wells or basins are used, and are often located in the sahn or courtyard. Wudu (small ritual ablution with water) is performed before prayers, as part of a process of achieving a state of ritual purity.
Calligraphy: from the earliest times the written word was used as the major, sometimes sole, type of mosque ornamentation, with total absence of figural decoration.
Dikka: wooden platform or tribune of single-storey height and positioned in line with the mihrab. Depending on size and climate, the dikka may be positioned in the courtyard outside. In large mosques where the imam is not visible by all, a mu'adhdhin praying from the dikka would help to keep prayers in unison.
Hypostyle: a type of mosque that is planned according to the basic unit or module of a rectangular bay defined by four columns or piers. The covered spaces of the hypostyle mosque consist of multiples of the basic module. The result is usually a regular composition or covered areas placed within a rectangular outline and surrounding a rectangular court.
Kursi: lectern on which the Qur'an is placed and from which the qadi reads and recites.
Iwan: a vaulted hall or space, closed on three sides and open on one; typically a four-centered arch open to a courtyard.
Maqsúra: a reserved space, often fenced or elevated, often located in the front section of the mosque, for use by Caliph, sultan, king or governor; other maqsúras were used for individual study or lectures.
Mihrāb: the niche that indicates the direction of prayer to Mecca (qibla), the spiritual focus of the mosque.
Minaret: principal vertical feature of most mosques, provides a local landmark as well as allowing the voice of the muezzin to carry over a considerable distance when calling the faithful to prayer.
Minbar: the pulpit, located on the right side of the mihrāb. It takes the form of a steep staircase, usually with a full balustrade, leading to a small, canopied platform. The imam leading the prayers reads or speaks from the step bellow the top platform, which is symbolically reserved for the Prophet.
Muqarnas: complex three-dimensional geometry present in vaulting.
Musalla: literally a place where prayer is performed, but has now come to mean a large, open-air place for communal prayer, typically outside the city; holiday or festival mosque.
Pishtaq: monumental portal forming the open side of an iwan.
Pool: may include a fountain and may be intended for ablutions before prayers, but is often decorative.
Portal: a central portal is a prominent feature of major mosques. General characteristic of architecture in the Muslim world is the concealment of the interior of a building from outside view.
Riwāq: portico or open arcades, usually along one side of a sahn.
Qibla: the direction that should be faced in Muslim prayer
Qibla wall: the wall perpendicular to the direction of Mecca, in which the mihrab is located
Sahn: courtyard, often surrounded on three of its sides by colonnades or arcades (riwaqs).
Ziyada: an enclosure around, or an extension of a mosque

Studio Work

01 "PRAYGROUND"

These designs are morphologically referential with respect to a ground on which they are grounded, suspended, or entrenched. The "ground" is both literal and metaphorical (that is the sacred ground) at the same time, instilling the "religious" with a notion of the earthly and the heavenly all in the same space. The students used different programmatic insertions, transforming museums, libraries, and spas into the surrogate religious institutions of our age.

ERIN DWYER

SUSPENDED BELIEF

The intent of this project is to create a charged and meaningful space at the intersection of two seemingly disparate programs — mosque and multimedia campus — thereby testing the studio's main premise that a formally and programmatically "expanded Mosque" can lead to the development of a contemporary religious Islamic space, one that fuses earthly experience with a meditative quality. In a part of the world that is still deeply entrenched in religious beliefs, this project offers a hopeful solution for the possible integration of a secular program in a religious space. While maintaining the autonomy of each in one simple and powerful architectural solution, this design confirms that the inevitable secularization of modern society does not need to necessarily oppose or expel the notion of the sacred.

The choice of a multimedia program comes from an interest in enabling the transparent convection of information within a relatively closed media culture, whether it be religious, political, cultural, or social in nature. If we are to imagine a new typology for worship, perhaps it is appropriate to envision a parallel evolution in the way current media shapes both our understanding of the world and our built environment. Creating a media-based cultural nucleus within Tripoli, which still holds geographic importance both on the coast and along the main artery between Lebanon and Syria, can help to redefine the city, recharge Niemeyer's fair complex, and spur new development.

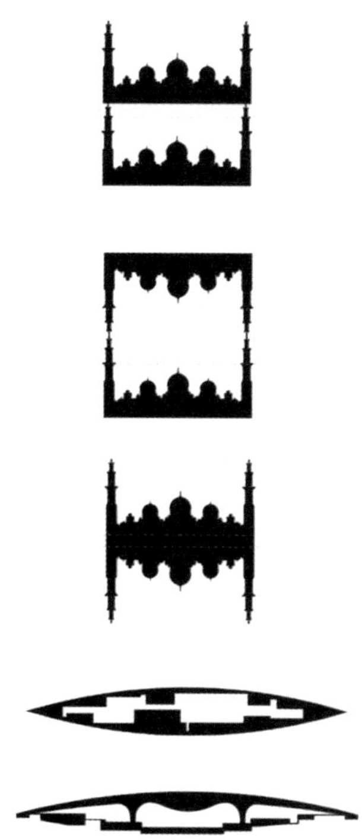

01 01

Spatially, this design attempts to define the mosque and multimedia center programs individually while also creating a visible relationship between them. By taking the typological courtyard mosque and turning it on its side, a tripartite parti of solid-void-solid is established, activating a dialogue between the two programs. Both the lower-level multimedia center and upper-level mosque share a formal language of pixelization derived from an interest in the part-to-whole rela-

01.01 Concept diagrams: The traditional courtyard is turned on its side and becomes a sectional void.

01.02 Site plan.

01 02

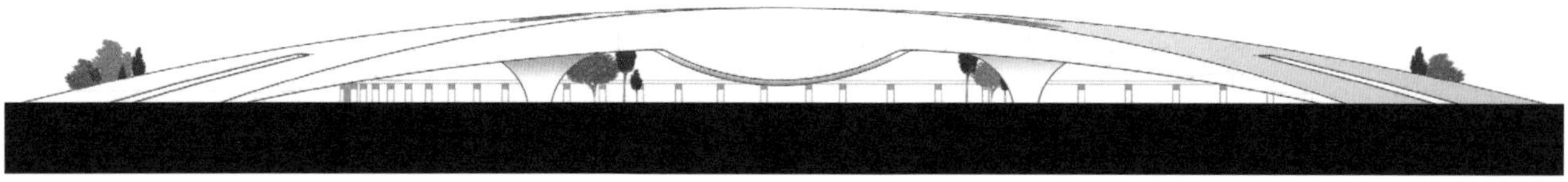

01 03

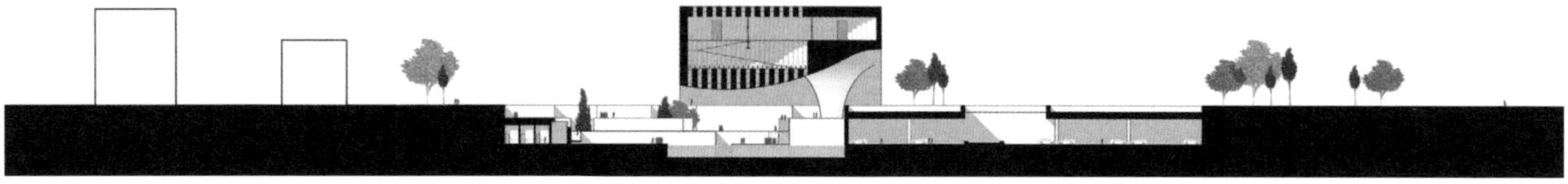

01 04

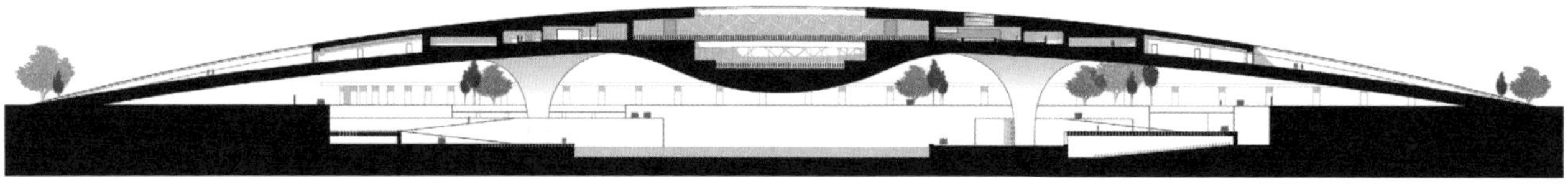

01 05

tionship of individual and communal worship, realized below in a series of stepped terraces that fall from Niemeyer's park to a central reflecting pool. Within these volumes are hidden public projection theaters, a digital archive, a gallery, personal viewing facilities, internet point, and meeting spaces. On top of these volumes, casual interaction hubs around a large, central projection wall showcasing public films or live broadcasts. Above, the mosque hides within the poché of an arched urban bridge, announcing itself in the subtracted dome and minaret forms along the structure's belly. The interior carved radial volumes of the mosque are also pixelized, with orthogonally stepped walls in plan instead of smooth curved surfaces. The two landscapes are further linked by the reflection bouncing between the polished copper panels on the underside of the mosque and the water of the pool below. Visual registration is limited to the z-axis, with apertures occurring at either the ceiling or floor.

Within the mosque, a prayer rug is made from light using an alternating rhythm of solid, and void, along the floor, divided by structure within each floor slit and by recessed lights within each solid band. As each person looks down, forward, and upward at points in the prayer ritual, they experience views which are singular to them because of the floor and ceiling divisions, creating a dual experience that is both personal and communal.

From the macro to the micro scale, this scheme aspires to create an experience of individual and collective development, fostering personal, cultural, national, and spiritual growth.

01.03 South elevation.

01.04 Cross section through the mosque, reflecting pool, multimedia program, and underground parking.

01.05 Longitudinal section through the mosque, reflecting pool, and multimedia programs.

01.06 Model vignettes highlighting slitted apertures and reflectivity.

01.07 Mosque program, terrace-level projection program, and lower-level multimedia program.

01 06

01 07

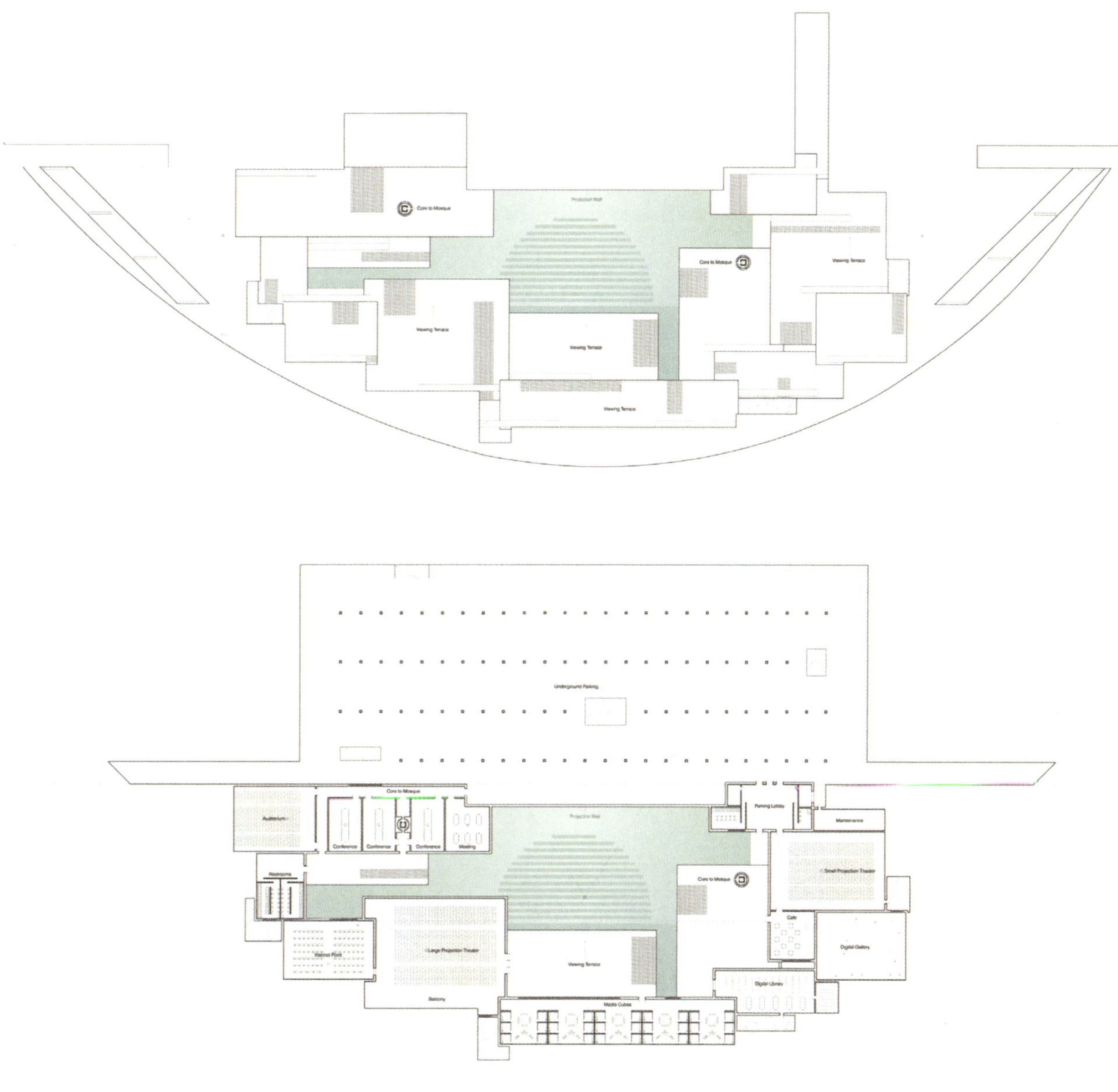

SEOYOUNG SHIN

MOSQUE IN WATER

The archetype of the mosque in the contemporary era has evolved not only as an exclusive prostration space for Muslims but also as an altruistic gathering space for the general public. This proposed hybrid mosque attempts to achieve a new understanding of the relationship between the mosque and water. The design couples the mosque with various types of water programs in order to create religious and leisure spaces. Since Islamic culture and religion give great significance to water, the mosque incorporates a series of ablution spaces as well as pools, *hammams*, and a public waterfall in order to redefine the boundary between and underline the co-existence of sacred and secular spaces.

The site in Tripoli, Lebanon, was part of the Babylonian Empire from 606 B.C. to 536 B.C. After the fall of Babylon, a period of Arabization and Islamification followed, and the empire dissolved into an Islamic province. Both Islamic and Babylonian cultures believed that life began with water. Their understanding of the universe was that it was surrounded by a series of water layers, which are layers of heaven. Following these ideals, the mosque is covered by cascading water and water spaces that suggest three types of ablution required for purification before carrying out religious duties. There are three different types of ablution spaces in this mosque: *ghusl* (complete ablution), which is located next to the prayer hall; *wudooh* (partial ablution), which falls from the top surface to the lower level; and *tayammum* (dry ablution), which is alongside the promenade on the top surface. There are two types of columns within the prayer space: the first type of column serves as a water collector in order to circulate and recycle the water from the top surface; the second type of collector acts as a light diffuser that creates a better quality of light in the mosque below.

02.01 Three types of ablution: *ghusl* (complete ablution), *wudooh* (partial ablution), and *tayammum* (dry ablution).

02.02 From left: the top surface with cascade and pools, two mosque prayer halls, and a parking lot.

02 01

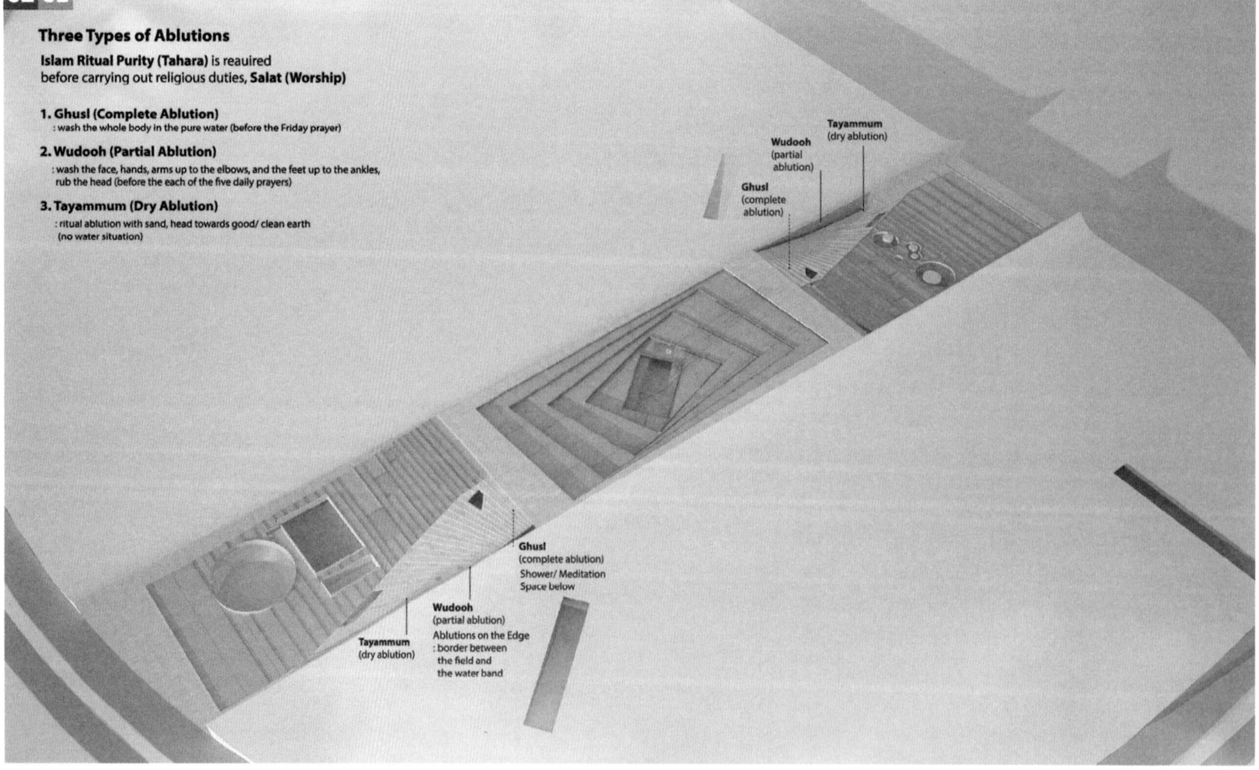

02 03

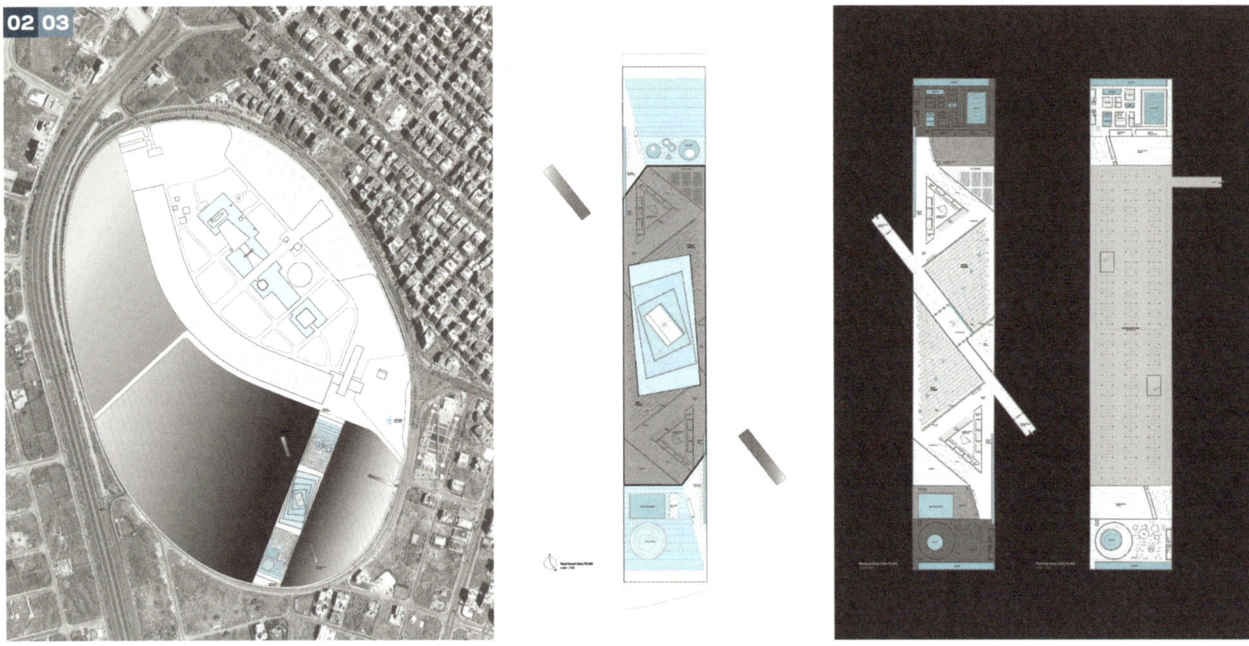

02 04

02 05

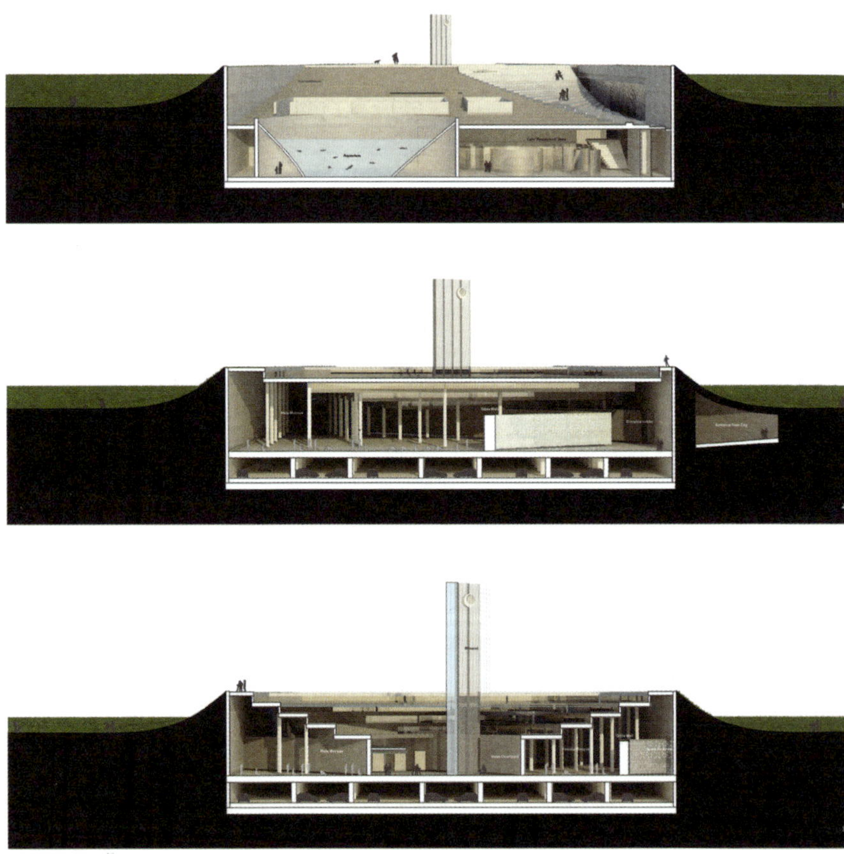

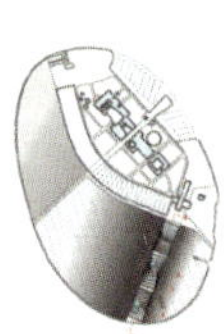

SECTION
scale 1:200

The mosque is located at the boundary between the old and new city, poor and wealthy neighborhoods, and the landscape and the built environment. The adjacent, expansive International Fair site, which includes various pavilions and water features designed by Oscar Niemeyer, also has an interesting water-to-building relationship. This relationship is inverted from the fair's "shallow body of water within buildings" to the mosque's "building within various depths of water."

The mosque promenade is gently inserted into the existing park adjacent to the fair. The top surface of the mosque is used as a continuous promenade that connects the fair to the new city districts. The cascade and the promenade provide a sense of sacredness and sanctity apart from the everyday, secular space. While wandering about the promenade, one experiences various types of water features, from a sacred waterfall minaret to leisure pools. The outer boundary of the promenade suggests a connection to the fair, and the very inner courtyard of the mosque indicates the axis toward the Mecca. The seven layers of twisting steps mediate the boundary of the surrounding secular life and the inner sacred space of the mosque. Reaching the top of the promenade, one is exposed to a panorama of Tripoli's cityscape and park as well as the mosque's water features and minaret.

02.03 Site plan at 1:1500 scale; pool-level plan (+4m) at 1:500 scale; mosque level plan (0m) at 1:500 plan; parking-level plan (-4m) at 1:500 scale.

02.04 Longitudinal section is rendered at a 1:200 scale.

02.05 Cross section is rendered at a 1:200 scale.

02.06 Mosque prayer hall under the cascade.

ANNE MASON KEMPER
LINEAR MOSQUE

This concept for a mosque and library on the expansive site of Niemeyer's abandoned international fairgrounds in Tripoli, Lebanon, begins from the hypothesis that the most ideal distribution of people in a mosque, as a space of non-hierarchical prayer, takes the same form as the most ideal configuration of books shelved in sequence: an infinite line. An analysis of the proportion, orientation, figure-ground, grain, and division of space in the traditional hypostyle mosque revealed a trend toward a horizontal, shallow, rectilinear prayer hall, with the long dimension corresponding to the *qibla* wall, the wall of the mosque perpendicular to the direction of the *Kaaba* in Mecca, that is faced during prayer.

Taking the form of a single, linear cut through the widest portion of the given site with regard to the direction of the *Kaaba* in Mecca, the *qibla* wall, designed as a wall of books, becomes the primary interface between the two programs. It is a manifestation of multiple traditions of text as abstract ornament; it calls upon both the Islamic precedent of non-representational calligraphic ornament and the Western precedent of ornamental text(s) in the modern library, from the façade of the Bibliothèque Sainte-Geneviève in Paris to the interior of the Beinecke Rare Book Library at Yale. The wall is at once a highly articulated plane upon which to focus during prayer and a repository for a collection of books, much needed in a country with no national library.

The line is a prime feature of the landscape, which intersects the existing buildings of the fairground, repurposed to house departments of a national library, including general stacks, a mediathèque, a children's library, and an auditorium. The line itself has a specific thickness determined by the width of the shelving containing the library's collection of religious texts, the length of a prayer rug, and circulation on either side. To accommodate more than 1,500 worshippers so that they can fit side-by-side along the length of the line within the fairground oval and to create a space for the library's reading room, the line inflates where the space of the site allows it, creating additional prayer rows behind the first in the same way the traditional mosque would. Here, an excavated ground plane, a finite enclosure, and an infinite roof plane each independently confirm the orientation and continuity of the linear *qibla* wall but allow for a much-expanded interior program.

The ground steps down to the *qibla*-books wall on both sides, with the enclosure and roof differentiating spaces for a courtyard and prayer hall on the mosque side and a reading room on the library side; the width of the enclosure ring itself houses office and support programs for both the mosque and library. The mosque entry sequence — beginning either at ground level, along the line, or from below-ground parking — circulates through shoe-removal and ablution locations before feeding worshippers into the prayer line along the *qibla* wall. The roof reflects light off the curved surfaces of the light wells into both the prayer hall and reading room, with the ability to calibrate light levels in different areas. Moreover, these elements in the roof reinstate the non-hierarchical, space-dividing properties of the traditional hypostyle mosque, allowing each worshipper along the line to experience a more personal, human-scaled mosque within the expanse of collective space.

03.01 In the hybridized mosque-library, the *qibla* wall becomes a wall of books and is the focal point, as well as the point of tension, of both programs.

03.02 The line of worshippers cuts through the widest portion of the site and runs in the direction of Mecca but has the potential to establish a prayer-based infrastructure that could continue into the city. The line is segmented and has a thickness determined by the unit of the prayer rug, .75 m wide by 1.5 m long, as well as the dimension of the book storage.

03.03 Section perspective: Light reflects into the space via wells in the roof that share the non-hierarchical space-division properties of the traditional hypostyle.

03 01

03 02

03 03

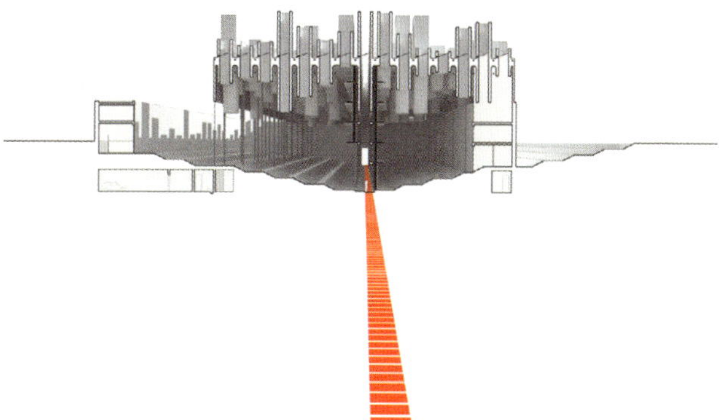

03 04

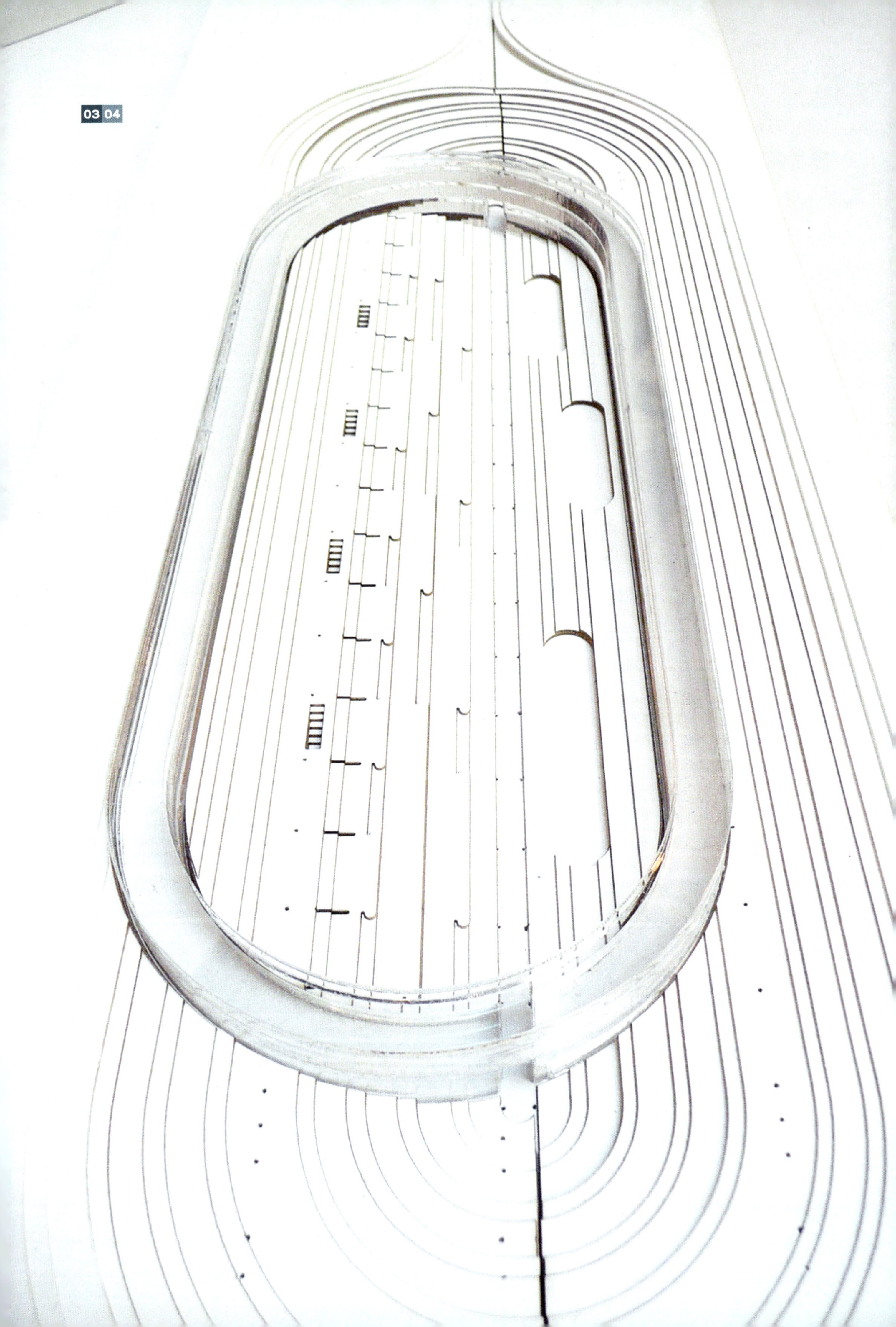

03 05

03 06

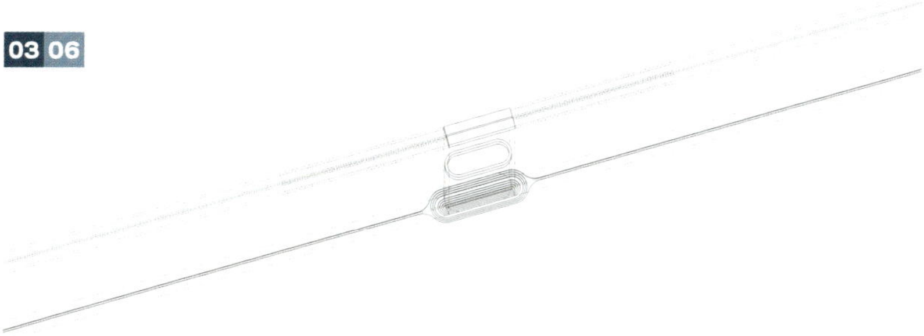

03 07

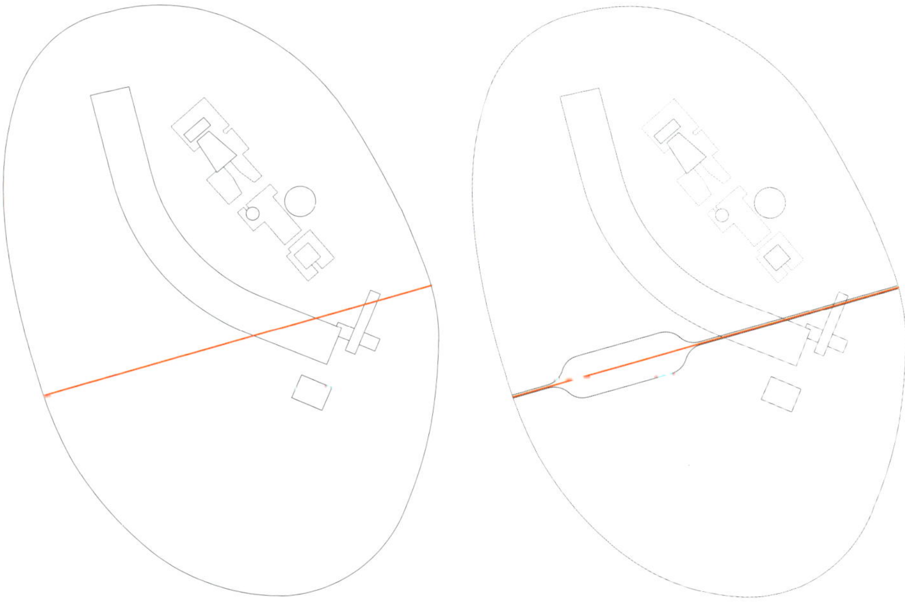

03.04 Ground enclosure: model is rendered at a 1:500 scale.

03.05 Ground: model is rendered at a 1:250 scale.

03.06 Three independent systems — ground, enclosure, and roof — come together where the line broadens, allowing this portion of the project to be simultaneously autonomous yet continuous with the length of the linear mosque.

03.07 In order to accommodate more worshippers, the line can inflate where the space of the site allows it, creating additional prayer rows behind the first in the same way a traditional mosque would.

LETÍCIA WOUK ALMINO

MUSEUM MOSQUE: ART IN PRAYER

The project conflates the mosque with the museum: the ancient Temple of God with the modern day Temple of Art. While the typical mosque consists of a central courtyard around which prayer spaces are located, here the main prayer space is in the center of the building, with the galleries occupying the perimeter and serving as a secular prelude into the sacred. Tension is created between the secular and the sacred as their respective spaces intersect, forcing the visitor to pass through the galleries in order to arrive at the final space of worship. The space of the museum functions like an ambulatory, a space of provocation and meditation at the scale of the individual, that is different from the collective spiritual experience taking place on the other side of the white walls.

The *qibla* wall, the surface toward which one prays, is marked by richly colored marble, which is set in contrast to the pure white walls of the museum. Inside the prayer hall, the worshippers focus their attention on the wall, which is illuminated by a shaft of light entering through skylights. On the other side of the wall, people gaze at the objects of art in the soft, even glow of the gallery.

The plan takes repeating geometric units to create four small prayer halls around the central space. Each prayer hall corresponds to a specific prayer time and a different quality of light, which is controlled by a complex grid of inverted skylights. Each of the six daily prayers correlates to a different prayer hall within the building. The skylights are modulated so that, at each specific prayer time, a bright slot of light shines directly on the *qibla* wall, indicating the focal point of worship. Thus, the movement of the sun throughout the day corresponds to the rotational movement of worshippers throughout the building. While the sacred spaces follow a changing daily cycle, the exhibition spaces are rotated on a monthly cycle. In this way, the Museum Mosque functions as a space for the translation of people but also of objects of art. It is a space of accumulation of people and objects but also of dislocation.

The size and aperture of the skylights correspond to the type of space below. Each space is shaped by the skylights. Sometimes, the skylights descend deep into the space and lightly hover above the ground; in this case, the skylight no longer functions as a skylight but as a water collector for the ablution rituals. In the larger prayer halls, the skylights become wide and deep, drawing long, dramatic shafts of light into the space. Light becomes sculptural and geometric like the shape of the ceiling, which is mirrored in the floor pattern as the reflected ceiling plan.

All the peripheral prayer spaces are enclosed, but the walls surrounding the large central prayer hall do not reach the ceiling, allowing sounds from inside the space to spill out into the galleries. The words of prayer resonate off the high ceiling and provide a musical backdrop to the viewing of art, conflating both experiences.

Lebanon is a country growing in its appreciation and collection of secular art. Beirut is often called the "Paris of the Middle East," but it is also marked by the strong presence of religious practices and rituals. The Museum Mosque attempts to create a dialectic between art and prayer, framing a view of the sacred from the perspective of the secular and vice versa. Through the precise manipulation of light and curated display of art, the building sets up a choreographed procession from museum to mosque.

04.01 The size and aperture of the skylights determine the program of the space below.

04.02 Each of the six daily prayers correlates to a different prayer hall within the building. The skylights are modulated so that, at each specific prayer time, a bright slot of light shines directly on the *qibla* wall, indicating the focal point of worship.

04 01

Mosque Hours

1. Fajr Prayer 04:42
2. Sunrise Prayer 06:04
3. Dhuhr Prayer 11:50
4. Asr Prayer 15:07
5. Maghrib Prayer 17:36
6. Isha Prayer 18:55

Friday Prayer 11:50

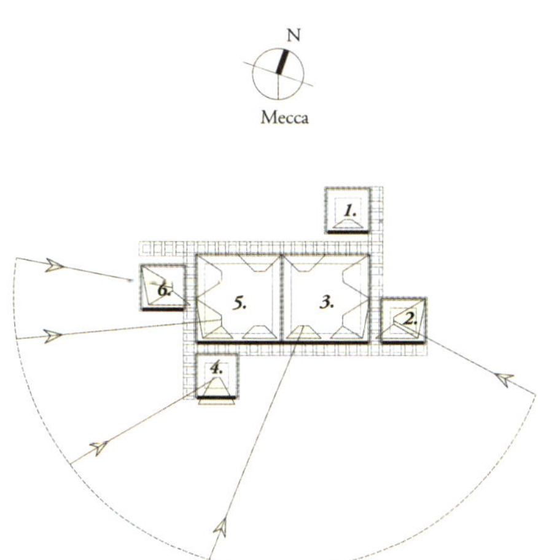

04 02

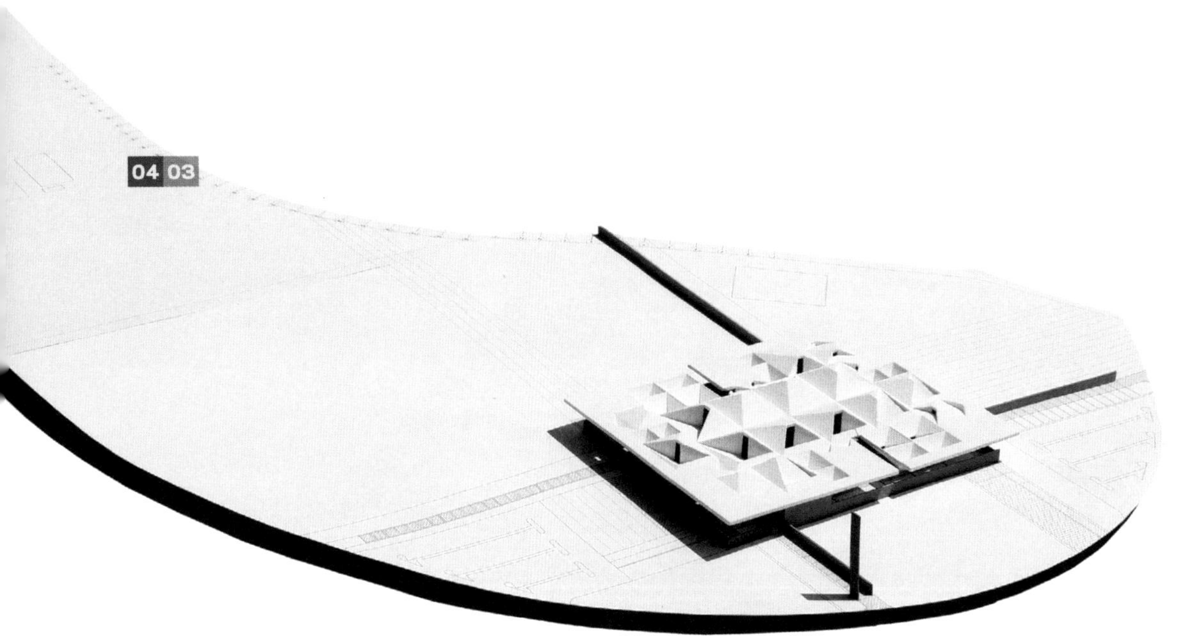

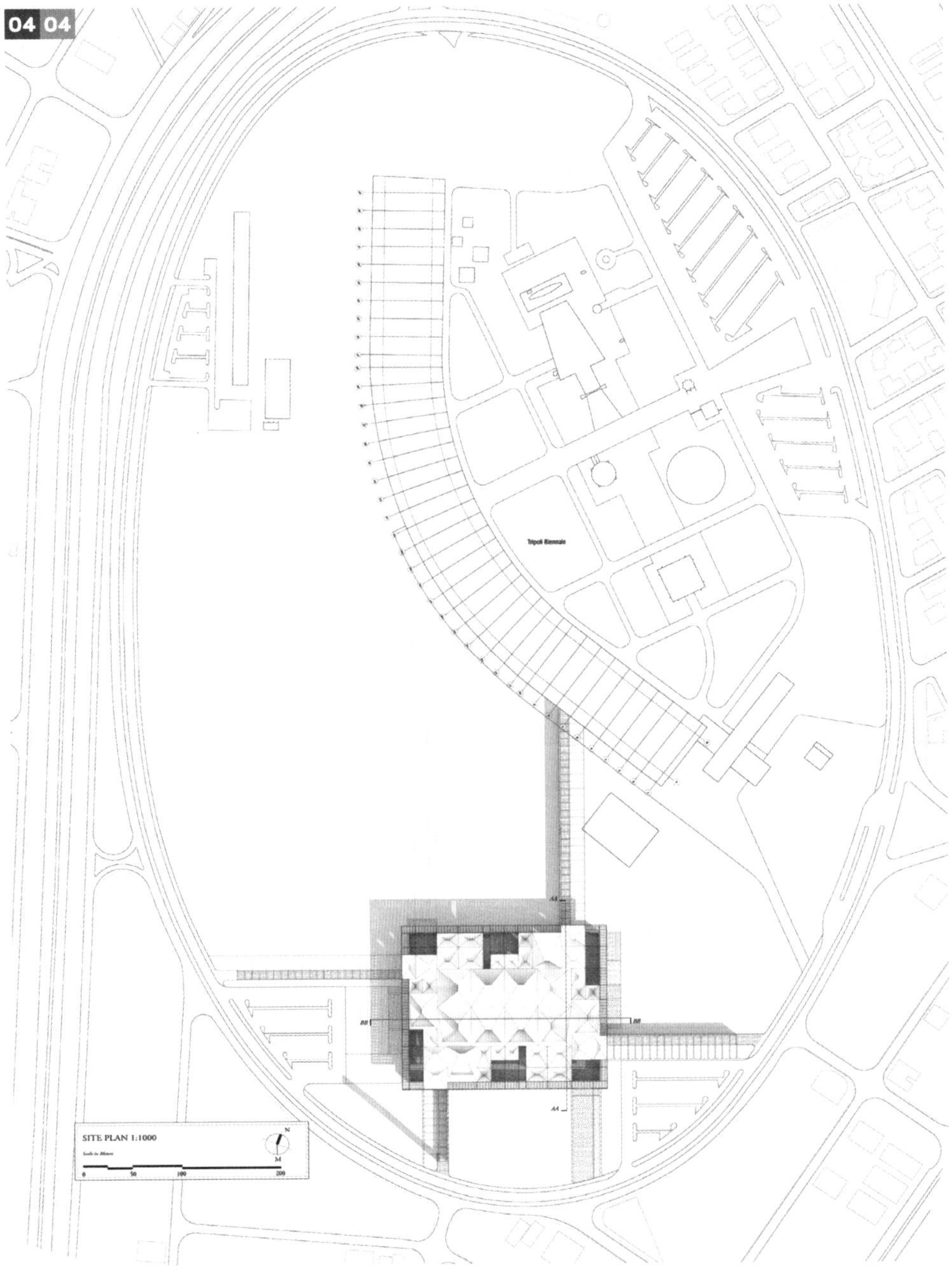

04.03 The roof plane hovers above the ground, while the walls extend out into the site, drawing visitors in through three points of entry.

04.04 The building sits at the southern edge of the site and has four points of entry that form a pinwheel path of circulation.

04.05 Light dips down through the inverted skylights, which form bright points of light within the space.

04.06 Museum section: museum-goers gaze at the artwork on the white walls.

04.07 Mosque section: Worshippers kneel in prayer toward the sumptuous marble *qibla* wall.

04.08 Drawing from the Arab graphic tradition of complex, repeating geometries, the plan takes a geometric unit that is mirrored and flipped to create four small prayer halls around the central space.

04 05

04 06

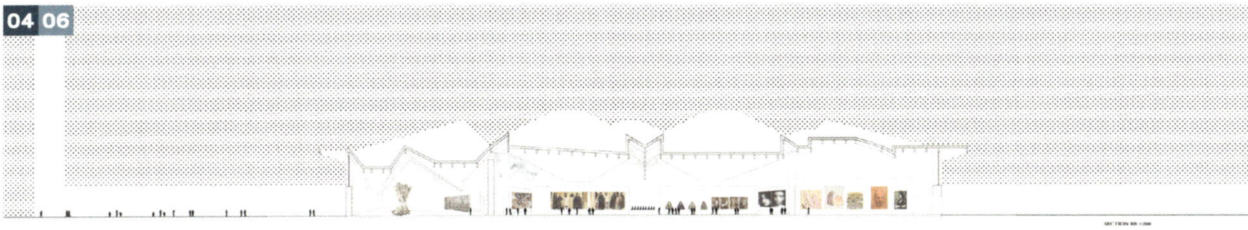

04 07

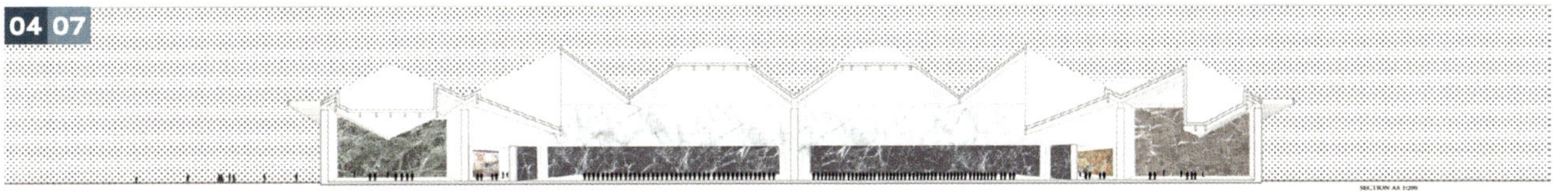

04 08

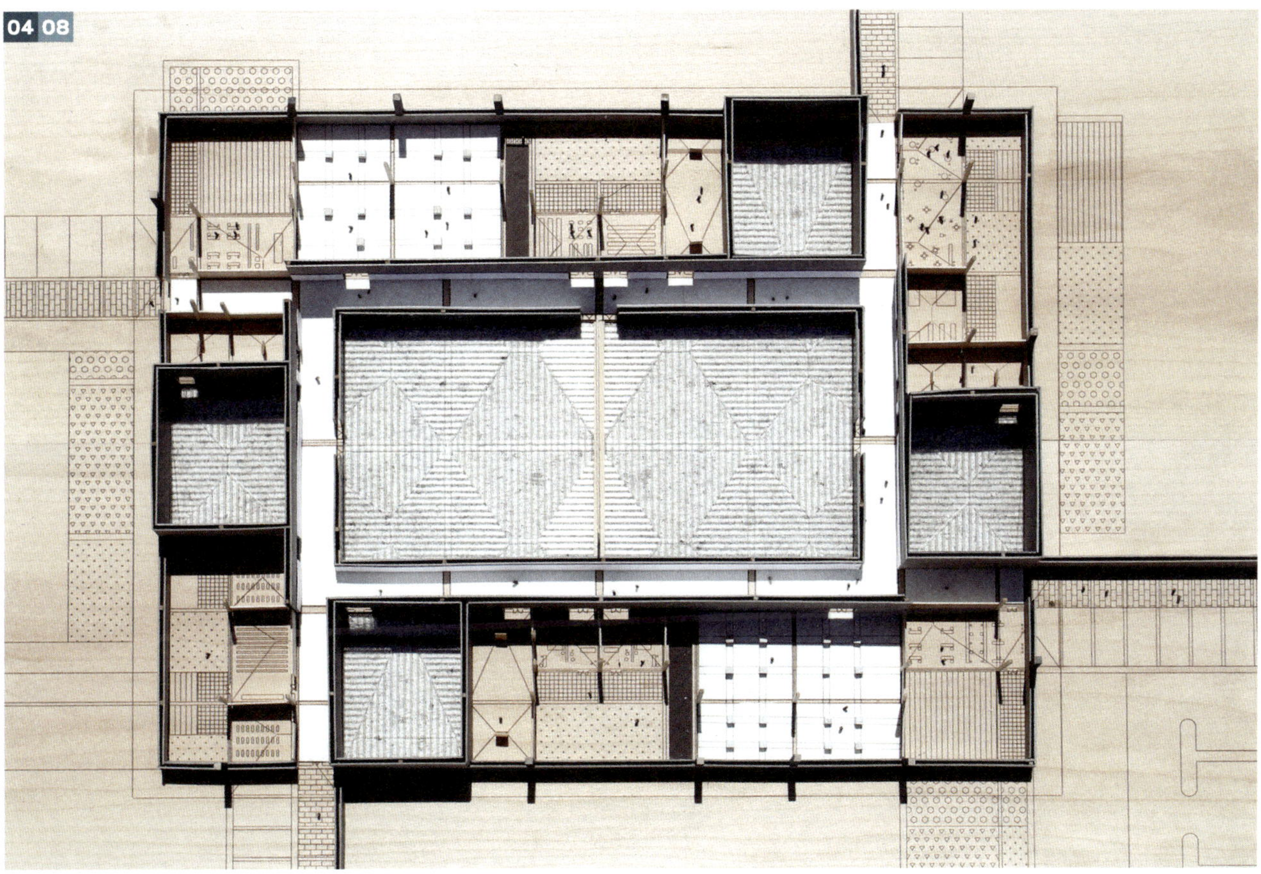

02 THE VIRTUOUS UBIQUITOUS

Employing plug-and-play conception of the mosque, the projects here understand the notion of the religious space not as a dogmatic ideology but as a fluid, mobile, transient "drive-thru" experience that shifts the "religious" from the sacred to the everyday by connecting it to the networks around us, from transportation networks to food and sports networks.

HILLARY BINGNEAR

FARM MOSQUE

Combining a mosque with an urban farm has the potential to not only preserve the site's openness when Tripoli's building density is increasing but also create economic stimulus with the mosque-urban farm's agricultural program of "produce, display, consume." Crops would be grown, bought, and eaten, all on site, by the 7,000 weekly worshippers. The landscape pattern, a combination of Islamic paradise-garden principles and practical pivot-point irrigation systems, creates an urban prayer rug. And just as mosques sometimes develop from the leftover space of an urban fabric, this mosque fits within the city's unused agricultural area.

For Friday prayer, the *muezzin* would call the worshippers to prayer from the minarets, which double as irrigation towers. There are six entryways, and all the paths within the site lead to the mosque. Worshippers would store their shoes and go to the ablution spaces. There are two ablution walls that look out onto the crops. The building is entirely transparent on the ground floor, allowing the landscape to be its ever-changing wallpaper. A series of ambulatory spaces surround the main prayer hall; tracks within the ceiling allow curtains to close off these spaces. The leftover programmatic spaces become light wells of varying depths and colors, creating the mosque's ornament. Some of these skylights open on the second floor, allowing sightlines between the two levels. The main prayer hall steps down in the direction of Mecca with a floating glass *mihrab* as its focus.

Overall, this proposal is meant to provide a simple, temporal, and ethereal space that is set in the agricultural landscape.

01.01 Site plan: Agricultural fields create the leftover space of the mosque.

01 01
Al Maarad
Riad El Solh
Bassel El Asad
Al Maarad
N

01 02

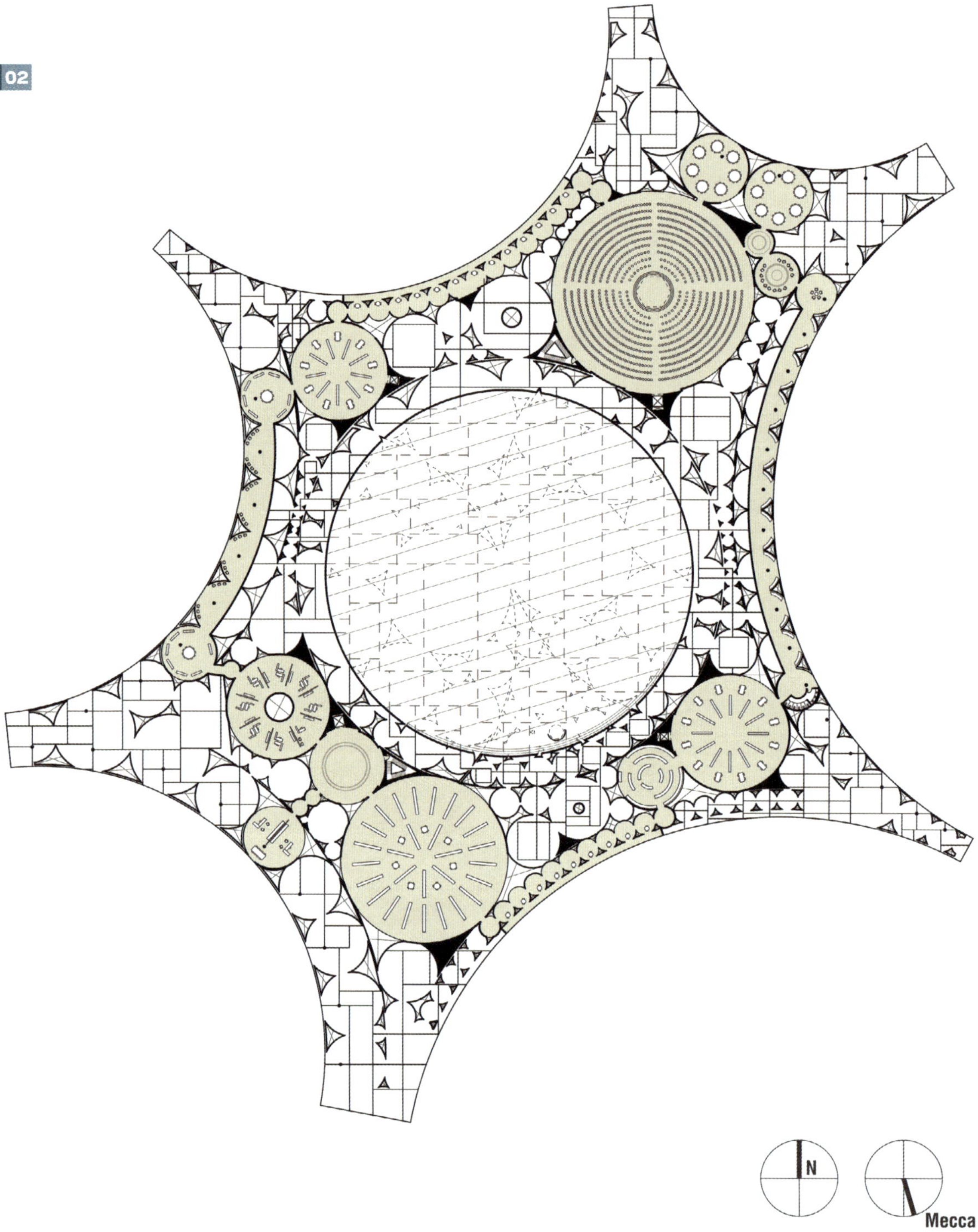

01 03

01 04

01 05

01 06

01.02 Level two plan: library, administration, and multi-purpose spaces.

01.03 Section through prayer hall and irrigation minarets.

01.04 "Leftover" skylights of varying depth and color create the mosque's ornamentation.

01.05 Worshippers walk by orange groves and wheat fields before entering the mosque.

01.06 Section model through prayer hall looking toward the *imam*.

MELISSA BAULD

TRANSPORTATION MOSQUE

This project proposes a new typology for the conventional mosque. It considers the unique spatial and social implications of a prayer hall overflow condition and, likewise, strives to linearly compose and colloquialize the mosque by pairing its program with that of a major transportation hub for the city of Tripoli. The transportation program includes a local and regional bus system, a regional train line with service to Syria and Beirut, and a ferry terminal accommodating regular trips to Beirut and Cyprus. While there is currently a bus system that provides connection between Tripoli and Beirut, a more efficient ferry route between the two cities would encourage stronger social and economic relationships, ultimately luring various businesses from Beirut to Tripoli. This way, rather than programming the Niemeyer fair itself, the Transportation Mosque serves as a mechanism to bring large amounts of people to the site, making it a national, even an international, hot spot.

The program of mosques as well as transportation hubs is governed by strict timetables. The Transportation Mosque consolidates the two schedules in order to increase the efficiency of Islamic prayer. All departure times are reconfigured to occur twenty minutes after each of the five daily prayers. Thus, people are able to arrive at the mosque for prayer and know they will be able to catch a train, bus, or ferry immediately following prayer.

Tripoli's Transportation Mosque is a singular point along which large networks of people are constantly in flux. The presence of prayer within the mosque creates a paradoxical pairing of active and stagnant programs. The program is organized around three oculi that draw light into the prayer hall and the two interior courtyards. Circulation occurs around these structural oculi-cones, a strategy which further emphasizes the proximity of activated space to those for repose and reflection. Interrelationships between the different programs are made through proximity and visual connections, rather than through pure hybridization, so as to not undervalue the sanctity or efficiency of either.

02.01 A collage depicting the infrastructural implications of the overflow condition of the mosque.

02.02 Transportation Mosque with Niemeyer's fair.

02 01

02 02

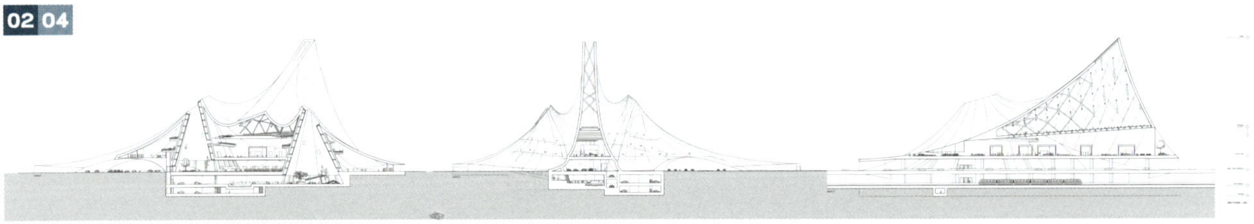

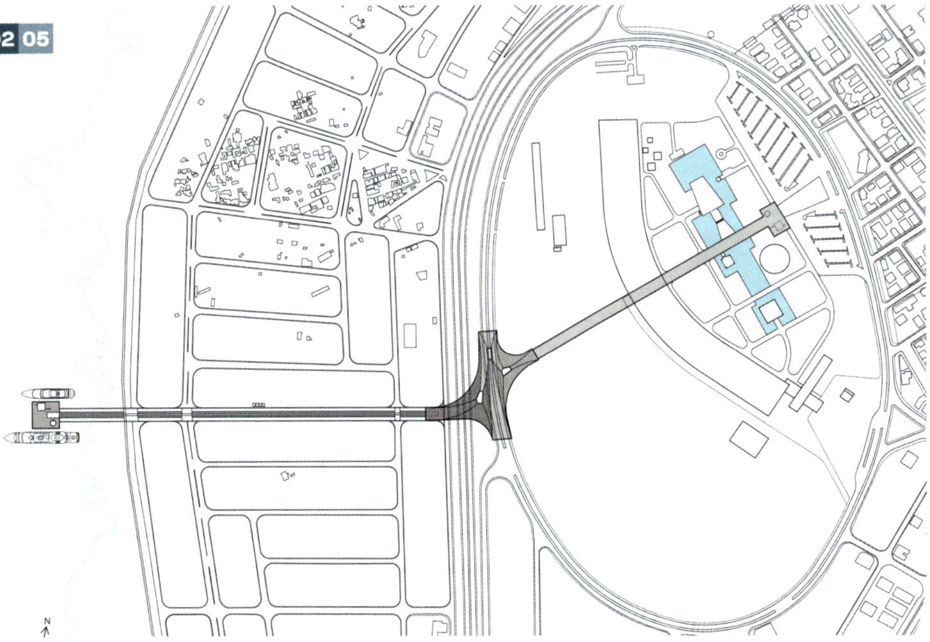

02.03 View inside the prayer hall.

02.04 Sections one, two and three.

02.05 Site plan.

02.06 Sectional model of the train station's courtyard and oculus-cone.

03 01

AMY CHANG
HYPOSTYLE-TRACK

The body in Islam is sacred, as the process of ritual ablution and the physicality of Muslim prayer attest. Yet, statistics show that Lebanon has the highest percentage of obese men and the third-highest percentage of obese women in the world. This project explores the hybridization of mosque and sports, using the organizational logic of the lane — recreational lane and prayer lane — as the point of intersection between the two programs. The expanded program becomes both the means for bridging the religious and the secular and the architectural provocation for rethinking traditional mosque typologies.

If in Arabic the word for "mosque" has the dual meaning of *masjid* and *jamee*, or the "place of prostration" and the "place of gathering" respectively, then this project seeks to expand through the strategy of gathering, the role of the mosque within the city. Athletics, sport fanaticism, and modern health culture are themselves religions of a sort and the means for activating Niemeyer's International Fair site. The oval is maintained as a recreational void within the fabric of the city, not unlike Manhattan's Central Park. Reprogrammed with sport courts and athletic facilities, the site becomes a cultural and economic amenity for the city of Tripoli, both a space for daily recreation as well as infrastructure for hosting large, international sporting events. Beirut has its marathon; Tripoli can now have its triathlon.

The master-plan strategy uses a running track (for running but also strolling, biking, and skating) to activate the entirety of the site through movement. The track takes advantage of Niemeyer's sweeping curves and creates a series of nested loops that make the runner continually orbit around, and return to, the mosque proper. The ritualistic circumambulation around the mosque recalls Islamic ritual at Mecca while maintaining a separation appropriate to each program.

The track extends to enter the mosque complex, which includes the prayer halls and their adjacent ablution spaces and *imam* and staff housing as well as a sports-training and swim center that share support facilities with the mosque. The geometric intersection of radial entry lanes and Mecca-oriented prayer lanes produces the generative grid for a dynamic hypostyle condition that defines the

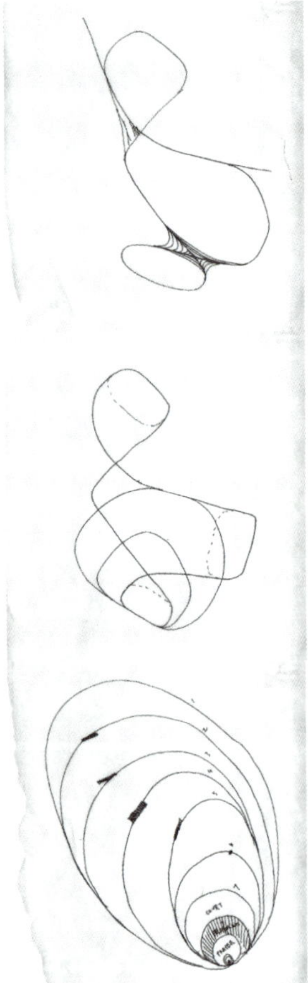

03 02

03.01 Interior view of the main prayer space.

03.02 Recreational track studies: the master plan proposes an overlay of looped and orbital, or nested, strategies.

03 04

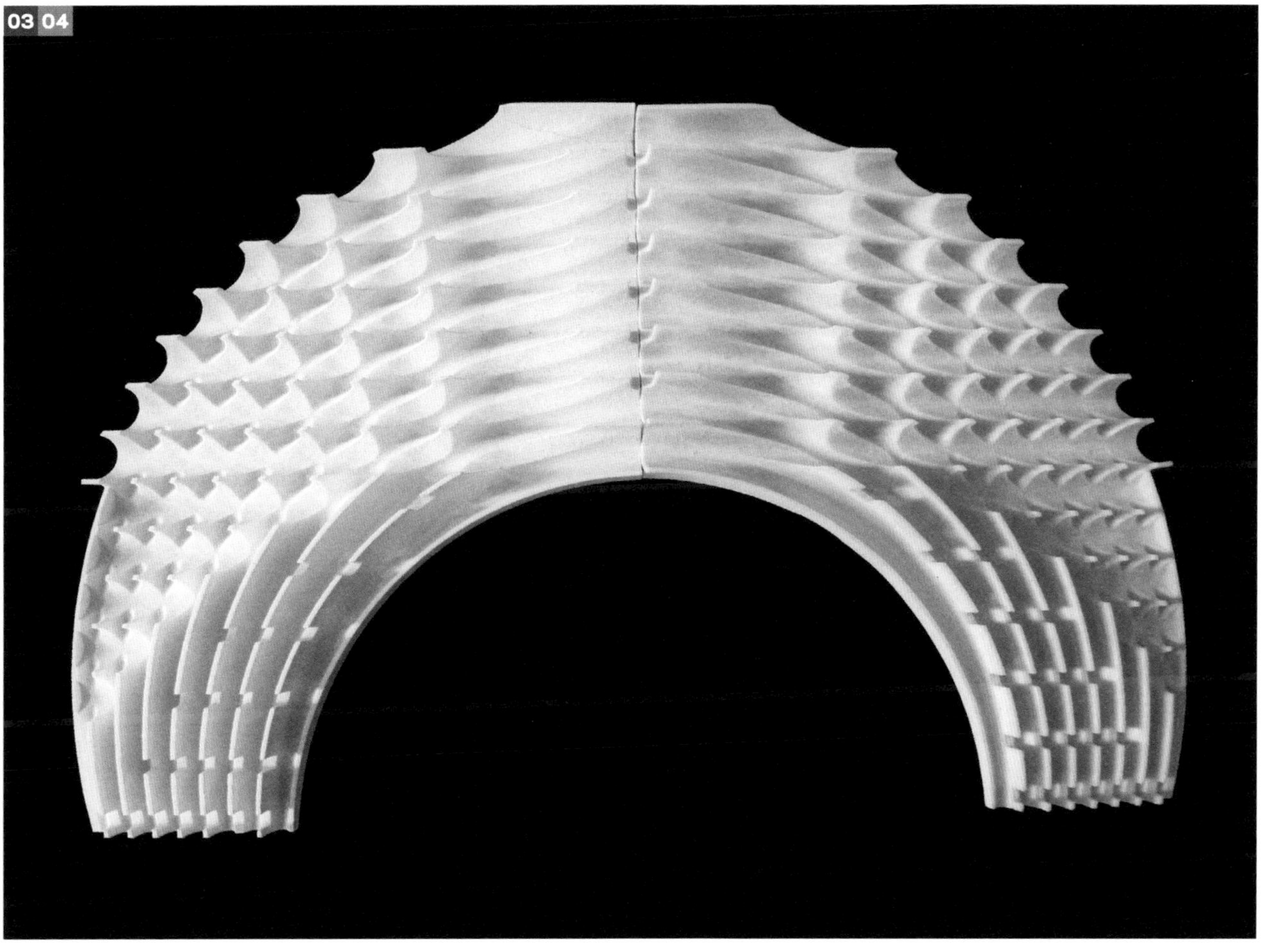

03.03 Sectional cut-away of the final model showing the inner courtyard; 1:500 scale plaster print.

03.04 Final model, underside, rendered in a plaster print at a 1:500 scale.

space for prayer. Essentially a "bending" of a traditional mosque prayer hall, the project speaks to precedent yet produces an architecture that is experientially and formally radical.

As the running and prayer lanes both suggest a rubber or carpeted material surface, it is the ground surface that is treated with material richness. The prayer hall is carpeted, and its saturated coloring contrasts with the simple materiality (whitewashed concrete) of the vaults, which are given subtle textural differentiation to distinguish the portions generated by either radial or parallel geometries. Small skylight apertures allow light into the prayer hall, while, at the perimeter, larger openings have layered screens to control light.

Symmetries in plan allow for a mirroring of male and female prayer halls. This doubling of prayer halls becomes a way to respect Islam's tradition of gender separation while legitimizing the female within the space of the mosque. This idea is architecturally reinforced by the geometry of the hypostyle, which creates a series of screening walls between the two spaces, providing visual separation while maintaining the mosque's open and continuous space.

The entirety of the complex takes on the landscape idea of a crater, allowing for a play of figure-void, object-landscape relationships. A sculpted berm, crescent in plan, surrounds the complex and alternately hides and reveals the mosque as one moves around it. A central courtyard, around which the prayer hall is wrapped, creates an experiential layering of horizon conditions with the existing backdrop of mountains and city.

03 06

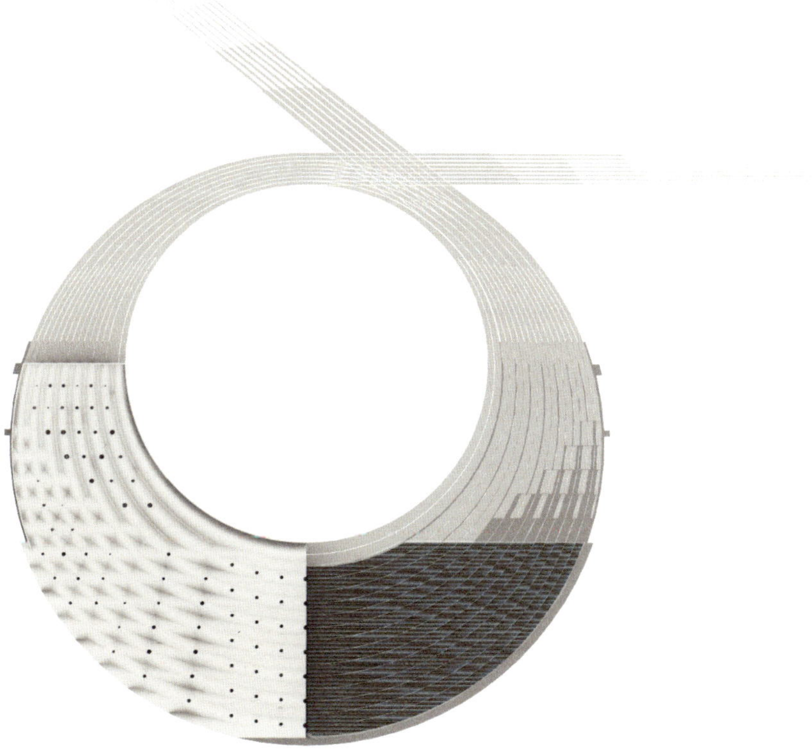

03 07

03.05 Close-up view of 1:1000 scale site model.

03.06 Final site model at a 1:1000 scale; Niemeyer's International Fair with the proposed mosque complex at right.

03.07 Material transition: the graphic of the lanes inverts as the pathways enter the complex, creating zones of transition into the sacred space. The prayer hall is carpeted with the generative grid of the vaulted geometry. The saturated coloring of the carpet contrasts with the simple materiality of the vaults.

03 PART TO HOLY

The proposals in this section deal with the metonymic understanding of religious spaces as elemental and typological dissociations/dissections that reference a greater whole. This fractal notion consolidates the different spatial components into a medley of one. The studio's Urban Qiblah Wall took the idea of the degree-zero mosque, or one's private home, as the premise to develop the mosque architecture as an index of the directionality to Mecca. The conflation of mosque and housing created a new typology of social housing in which, again, the "religious" potentially can be performed from the comfort of the domestic space.

DAVID TASMAN

COMMUNITY HOUSING MOSQUE

In 2007, prompted by a series of terrorist bombings by the Islamist militant organization Fatah al-Islam, the Lebanese Armed Forces destroyed the Nahr el-Bared camp, home to roughly 30,000 Palestinian refuges. Overnight, the population of the neighboring Beddawi refugee camp doubled, taking in those newly displaced. Today, the Beddawi camp remains congested and unable to provide adequate accommodation to those who seek shelter there.

01 01

Near the Beddawi camp, the 10,000 hectare site of the Rachid Karami International Fair, designed by Oscar Niemeyer, remains vacant, only occasionally used for walking and jogging by Tripoli's elite citizens. Meanwhile, overcrowding and poor housing conditions persist for tens of thousands in Tripoli.

This proposal seeks to awaken the dormant potential of the vacant fair by siting a new typology of housing combined with a large Friday mosque on the underused southern side of the fair. In traditional neighborhoods, women pray at home and men pray at the mosque. In this proposal, the neighborhood and the mosque are combined. The form of the housing creates the enclosure of the mosque so that the two programs are inextricably linked. The project is sited to activate the undeveloped southeastern sector of the fair. By introducing new arteries previously routed around the oval into the nucleus of the site, the housing compound creates a node of new activity. The park-like setting of the existing fair is preserved while the existing "boomerang" building of Niemeyer's design is re-envisioned as a school, providing education for those living in the new compound. The segment closest to the housing compound provides education for the youngest group, the middle segment for high school, and the farthest segment as a community college.

01.01 The interior space of the mosque is defined by the private balconies and *musallas*, which allow the residents above to pray from the privacy of their own apartment.

01.02 Concept collage illustrating the programmatic pairing of housing with a grand public mosque.

01.03 Plan diagrams show occupiable space.

01 02

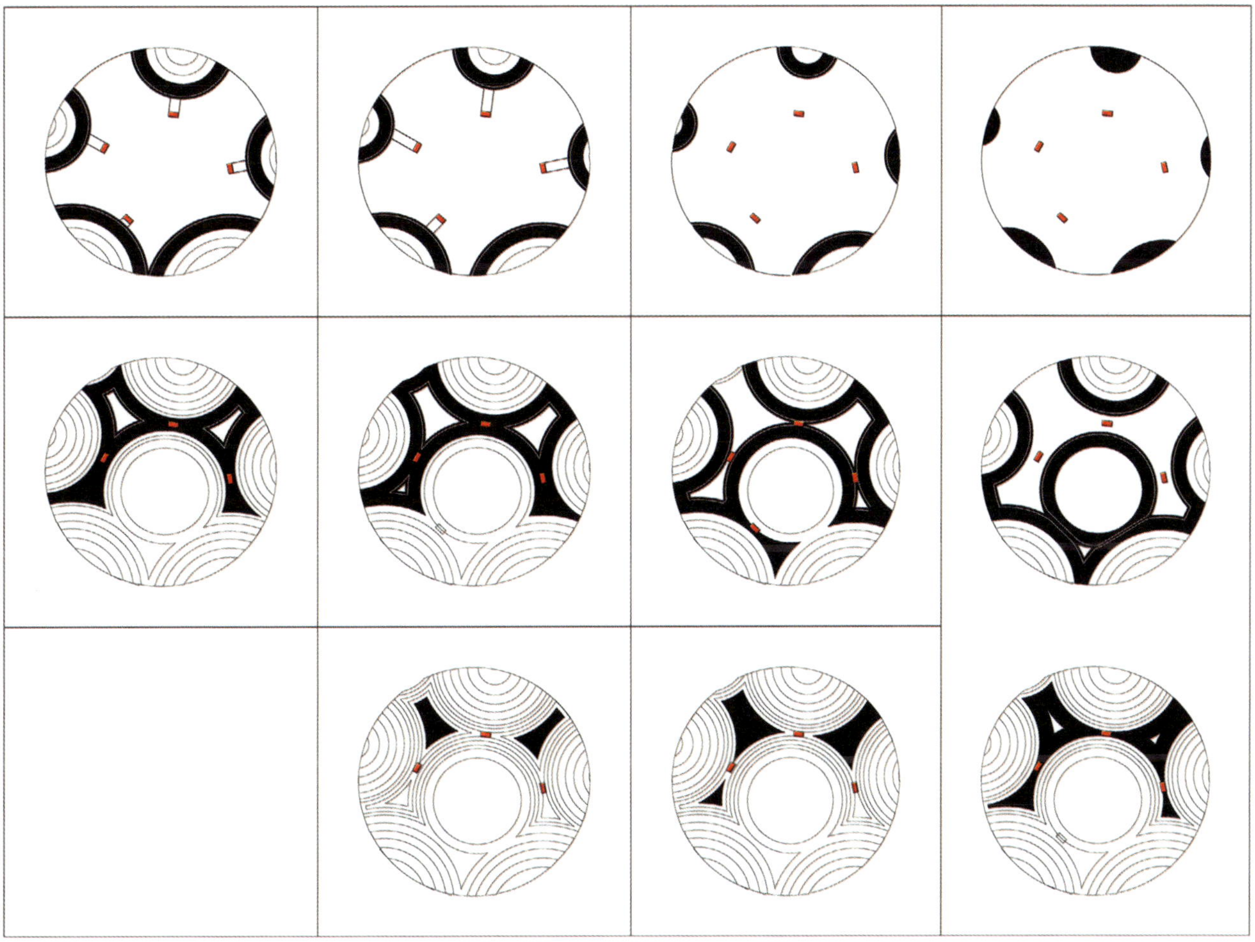

01 03

01 04

The mosque is located at the center of the housing project, with the *qibla* wall facing south toward Mecca, giving the project its orientation on the site. The traditional buffer zone between the mosque and the city is inverted and interiorized. Here, the *ziyada*, as the buffer zone is known, hosts a market on the ground floor, mitigating traffic into the apartments or into the mosque. A ring, rising several stories high, encloses the mosque and acts as a purifying membrane. It contains the ablution spaces, bathrooms, and also hides the elevator banks. The outside of the ring is smooth, while the inside is a rough composition of overhanging balconies that are reminiscent of *muqarnas*. On the upper levels, private balconies, or private *musallas*, overlooking the mosque, allow residents to pray in privacy. The upper level of the mosque is the first level that encircles the mosque without interruption, uniting the building in plan. This level also contains the apartment for the *imam*; public support spaces for the mosque, such as the library, gym, and conference center; and space for administration. Structurally, this top level doubles as a compression ring for the steel trusses that support the housing. Traditionally, an ornate chandelier is used to illuminate the mosque interior; here, the chandelier is recast at an architectural scale, forming the roof of the mosque while bringing natural light into the heart of the building. Gaps in the mat of apartment units also allow for light to stream into the space and enhance air circulation.

This new typology, which proposes the combination of neighborhood and mosque, provides an alternate image of contemporary Islamic architecture. It participates in the rich tradition of Islamic architectural principals while standing in strong juxtaposition to Islamic tradition in which women pray at home and only men pray at the mosque.

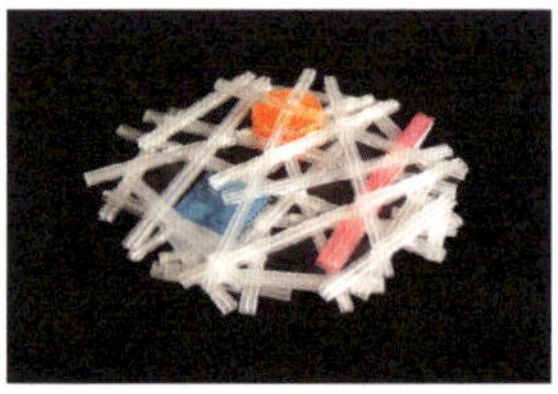

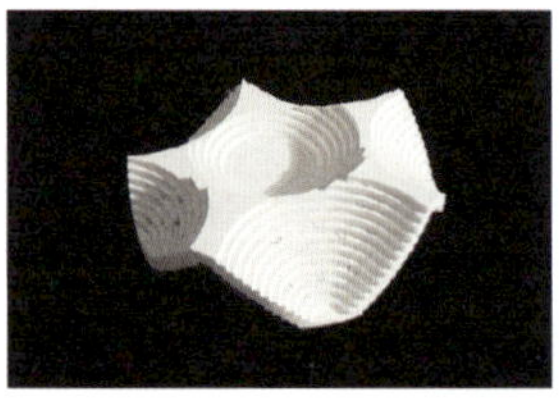

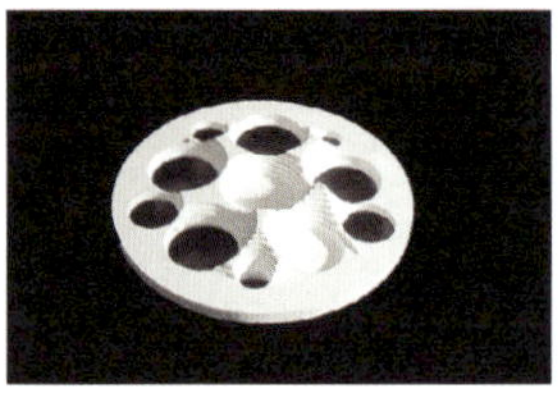

01 05

01.04 Model showing apartment variation and the public roof garden.

01.05 Study models.

RONALD LIM

THE SOL-URBAN QIBLA

This investigation into the mosque studies Islam's dual directionality. Not only must mosques be oriented to Mecca, but specific prayer times are measured by the sun's position in relation to the mosque. For example, besides the noon prayer time occurring at solar noon, the midday prayer time, Asr, is described by the Koran as the time when a shadow is twice the length of the height of the object casting the shadow. The result is a mosque in which these two directions (a pure north-south solar orientation and a *qibla* direction to Mecca) come together to inform the plan and approach. The interior prayer space allows direct sunlight exactly at solar noon, an important daily prayer time. The accompanying pool reflects the sun during the midday Asr prayer time.

Equally central to the project is that the mosque be an "Urban Qibla," indicating the prayer direction for the rest of the city. This idea was first explored in a photo collage exercise that considered devotees, during prayer, facing a monument of greater urban presence than the mosque's *qibla* wall. It acknowledges that inhabitants do not have to be in the mosque to faithfully commit to prayer; they can pray at home. This results in a mosque that has an urban-scale *qibla* wall that serves the rest of the city. The wall has a vertical slit at its minaret. At solar noon, sunlight passes through this slit to align with the approach path to the mosque.

02.01 Interior perspective showing direct sunlight in the prayer hall at noon prayer time.

02 02

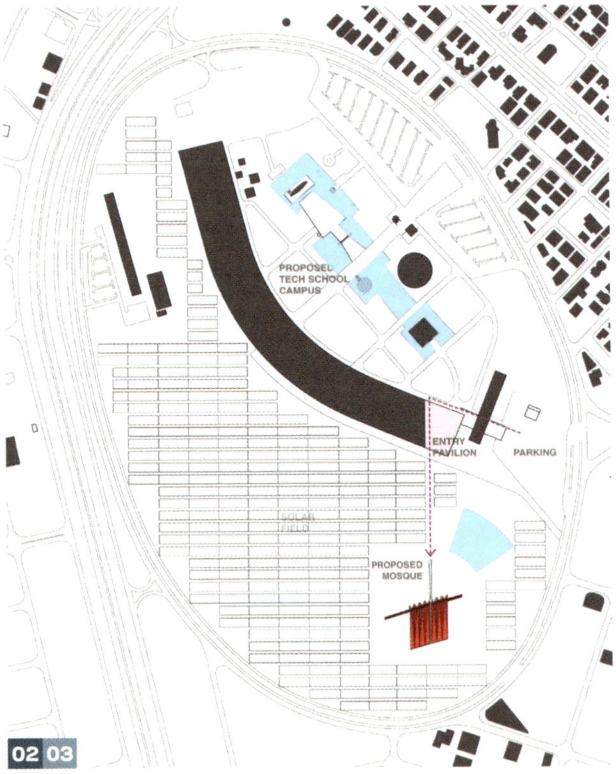

02 03

02 04

02.02 Early photo collage exercise exploring the idea of praying toward a *qibla* marker that has an urban presence.

02.03 Site plan indicates the location of an urban *qibla* mosque with a reflecting pool in a field of solar panels.

02.04 Exterior perspective view of mosque simulates solar conditions twenty minutes before noon prayer time, with the oculus' shadow and approach path almost aligned.

02.05 Section perspective.

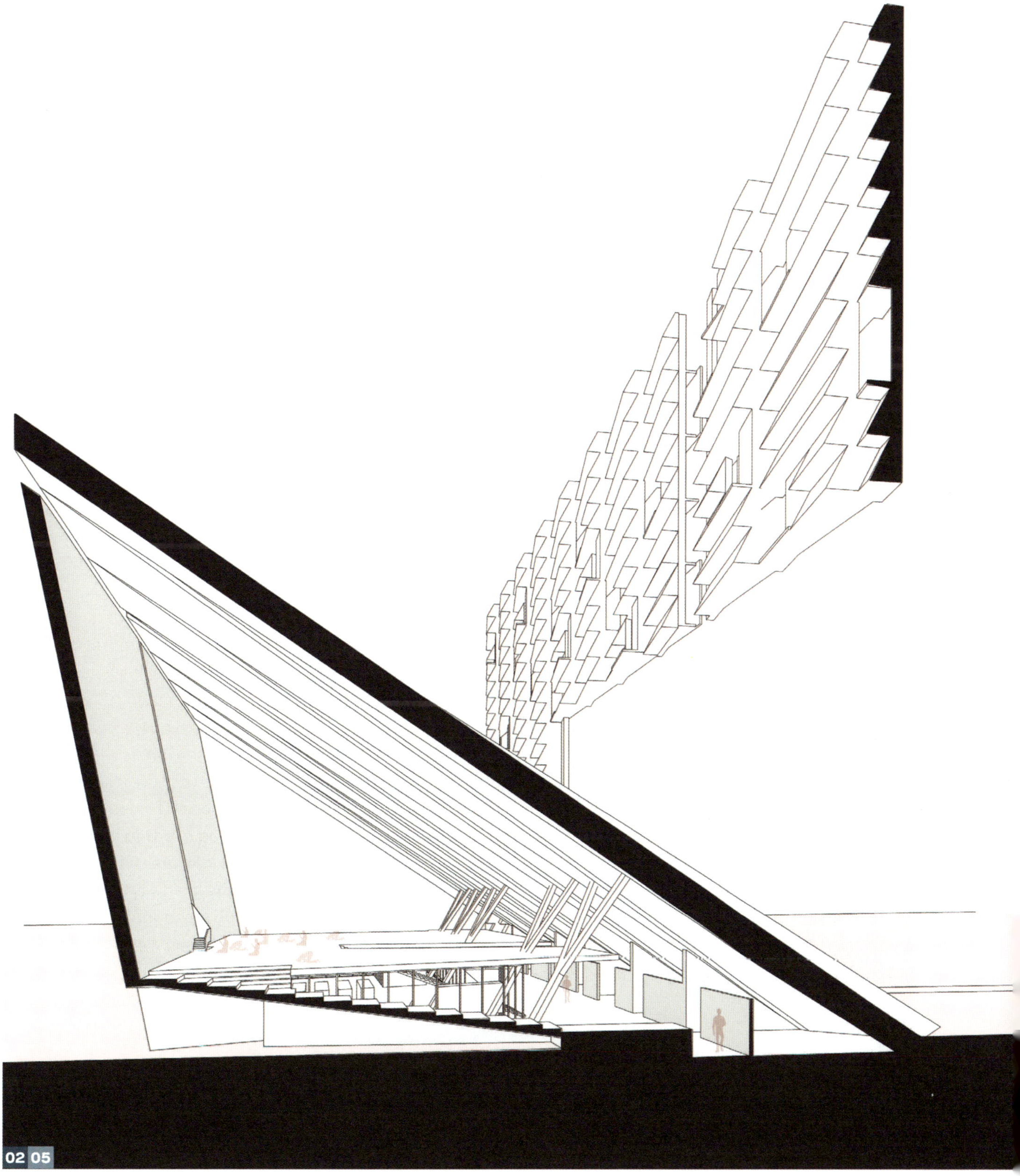

JACOB DUGOPOLSKI

TRI-POLIS ALLURE

Easily visible from the air and an impenetrable concrete barricade from the ground, Niemeyer's oval fairground is currently a fenced-off void that the city develops around. This project looks to incrementally open a connection with this valuable asset. The project's three main goals are to strengthen regional governance, provide and activate a necessary third city center with education and civic functions, and create a major mosque between these programs. Balancing religion (*din*) between the state (*dawla*) and the everyday (*dunya*) is an attempt to recapture the mosque's role as a community gathering space. Islamic scholar Mohammed Arkoun states that the mosque is a space of dialogue between these three "differentiated but articulated spaces in which all human existence has to unfold" (*Islamic Culture, Modernity, Architecture*, 1986). In reconstructing and reinvigorating the oval's edge, this combination has the potential to foster a new dialogue.

One of the reasons for slow growth in Tripoli is the lack of strong regional governance. Tripoli and its region of nothern Lebanon exhibit the lowest development indicators. By encapsulating offices, this site would be the foundation to develop and implement a regional plan. Tripoli has also been traditionally an important educational center, and a new branch for the Lebanese University has been pursued for the edge of the city. Expanding the political science branch (5,000 students) into the core of the city offers direct interaction with new government offices.

The oval was largely a leftover formality. Originally built on a square plot, the oval form came back in its current misaligned form as a result of the highway. Niemeyer opposed any fence, but the city walled off the grounds, keeping only a main entry to the southeast and a VIP entry to the northeast. People that know the guards from these high-rent apartment buildings on the eastern edge are

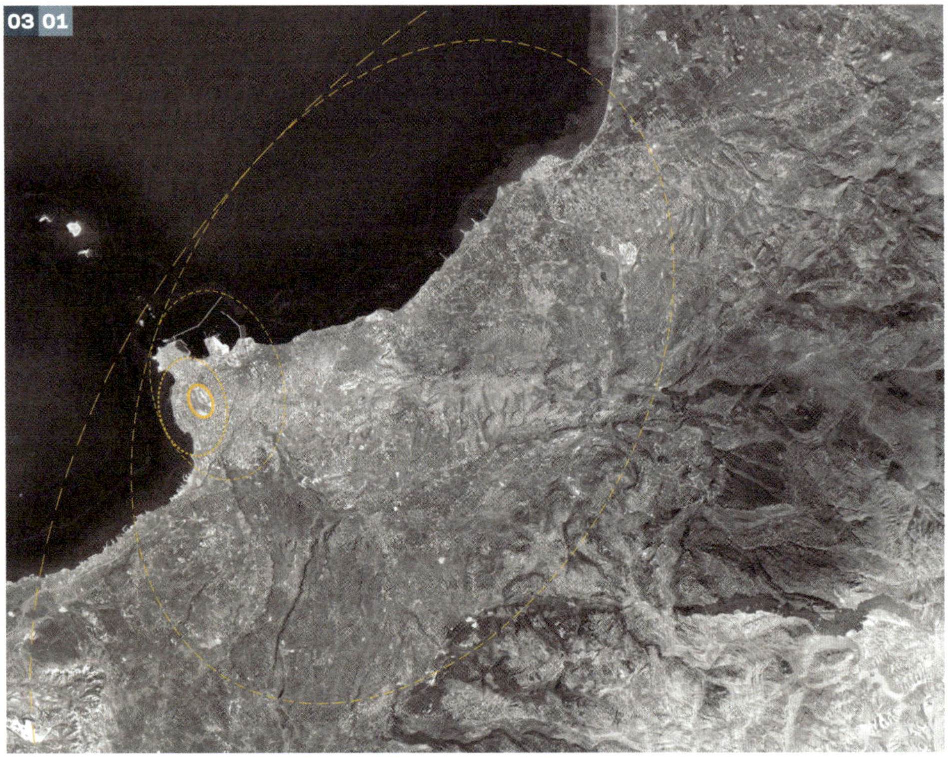

03.01 Aerial view of Tripoli showing the visibility of the fairground and its regional potential.

03.02 Site plan of the complete oval strategy showing the projected growth of buildings around the edge over time.

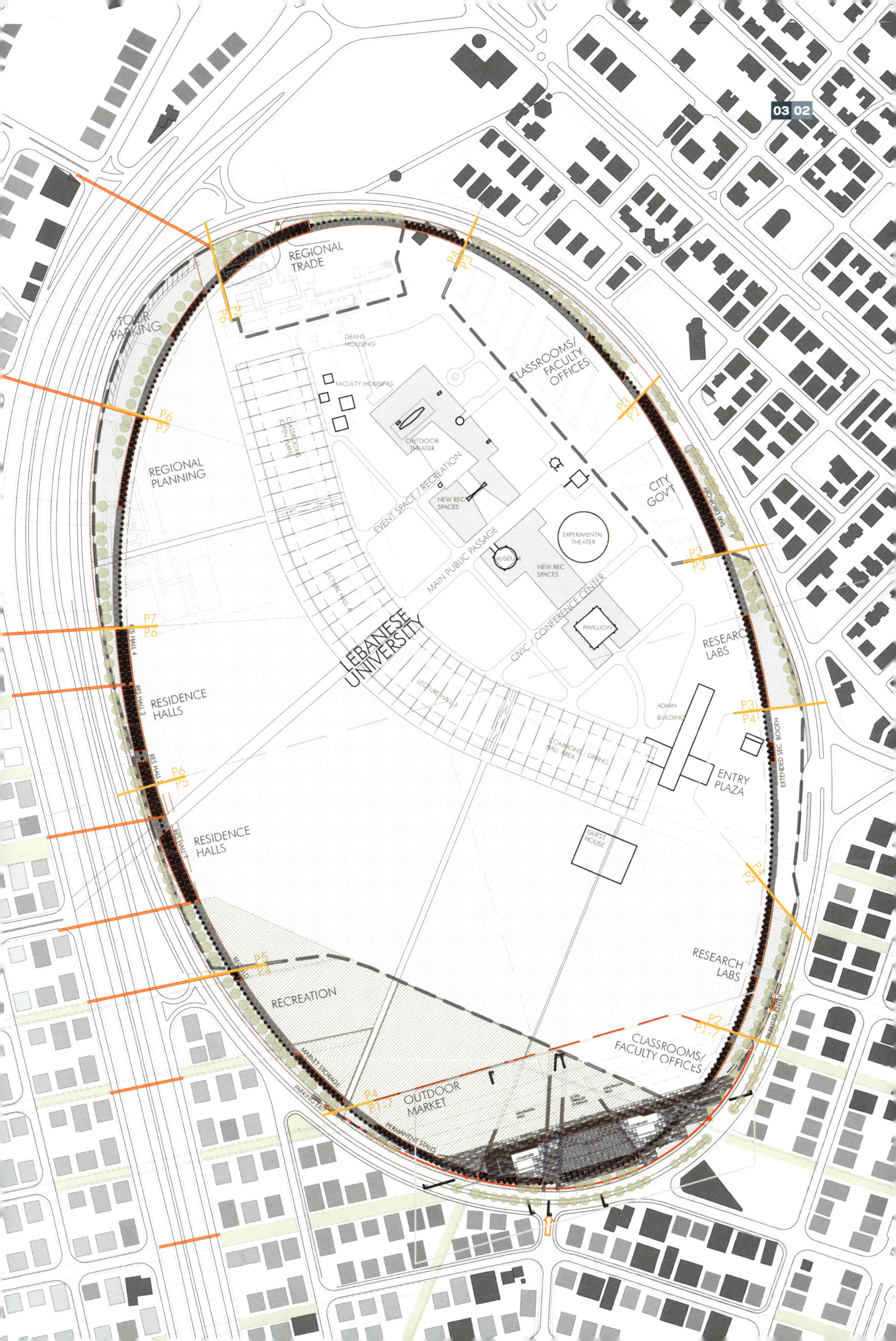
REGIONAL TRADE
TOUR PARKING
DEANS HOUSING
FACULTY HOUSING
CLASSROOMS/ FACULTY OFFICES
CLASSROOMS (OPEN PLAN)
OUTDOOR THEATER
REGIONAL PLANNING
EVENT SPACE / RECREATION
NEW REC SPACES
CITY GOV'T
TAXI DROP OFF
EXPERIMENTAL THEATER
MAIN PUBLIC PASSAGE
MUSEUM
NEW REC SPACES
LECTURE HALL 4
CIVIC / CONFERENCE CENTER
PAVILLION
LEBANESE UNIVERSITY
RESEARCH LABS
RES HALL 4
RES HALL 3
RESIDENCE HALLS
ADMIN BUILDING
LECTURE HALL 3
COMMONS HALL AREA / DINING
ENTRY PLAZA
EXTENDED SEC. BOOTH
RES HALL 2
RES HALL 1
RESIDENCE HALLS
GUEST HOUSE
RESEARCH LABS
RECREATION
PARKING ENTRY
CLASSROOMS/ FACULTY OFFICES
MARKET STORAGE
PARKING EXIT
OUTDOOR MARKET
PERMANENT STALLS
COURTYARD
P1
P2
P3
P4
P5
P6
P7
P1-7

covert users. Where the population is continuing to grow, there is a lack of access and connection to what this space can offer.

Currently, the oval is a popular ambulatory loop and could be enhanced to form a social space, such as the Beirut Corniche. The project's title refers to the definition of "allure" as a medieval wall walk and also to the attraction it could provide in a contemporary setting. Tripoli originally meant "triple city" in Greek. This proposal functions as a third city center of the contemporary conurbation. It does so in an inverse manner from El Mina and the Old City centers, which use geographical features to guide the main road and form distinct spines from which to build. Rather, this site uses the edge to activate the growing city and connect separate areas along the mile loop.

Slightly modifying the master plan, which was designed but not yet completed by the city, this proposal's view corridors and connections to the coastline are achieved by extending the sidewalks to become open landscape passages through the longitudinally oriented blocks adjacent to the site. Furthermore, the plan pulls grids into the site to create connections to Niemeyer's initial plan while also channeling flows to create new entrances.

03.03 Site model roof-and-edge strategy has a series of modules that shift in scale from the edge to the core.

03.04 Rendered perspective shows the central prayer area and the luminous glow emanating from the structural system.

03.05 This series of cross sections shows the sequence from the courtyard to the entrance and, finally, to the central prayer space.

03 04

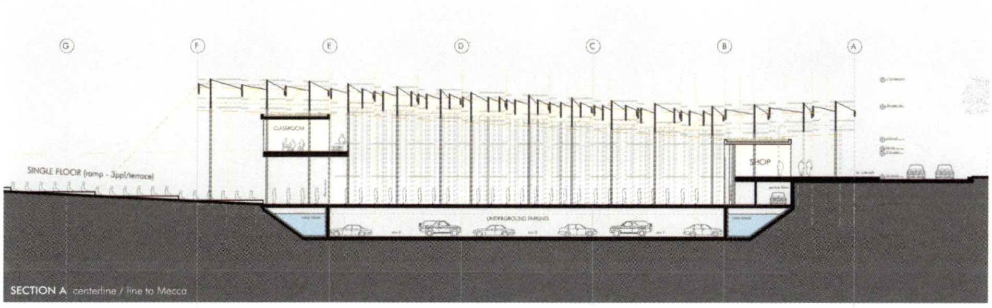
G
F
E
D
C
B
A
CLASSROOM
SHOP
SINGLE FLOOR (ramp - 3ppl/terrace)
UNDERGROUND PARKING
SECTION A centerline / line to Mecca

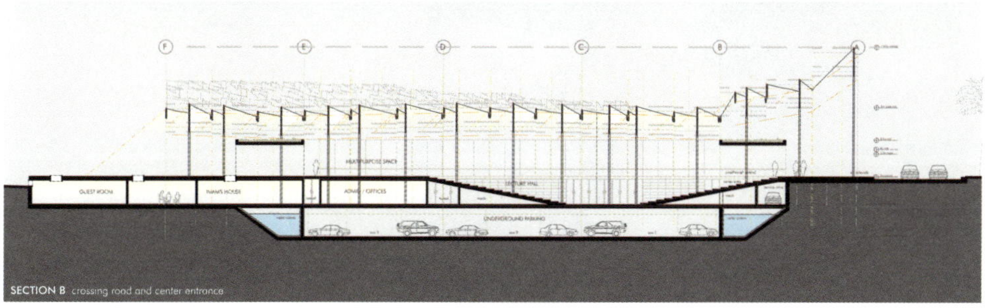
F
E
D
C
B
A
MULTIPURPOSE SPACE
GUEST ROOM
IMAM'S HOUSE
ADMIN / OFFICES
LECTURE HALL
UNDERGROUND PARKING
SECTION B crossing road and center entrance

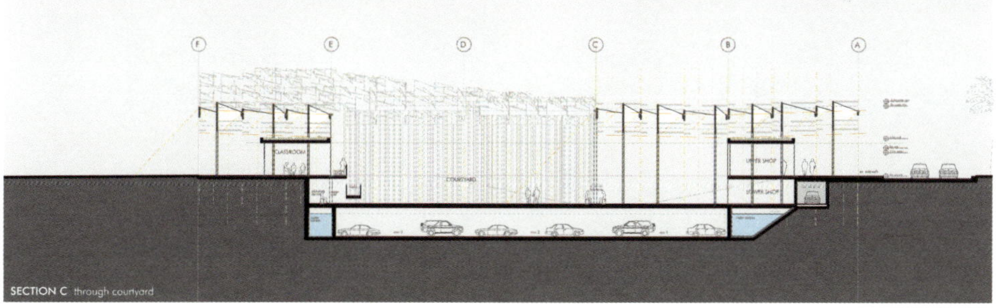
F
E
D
C
B
A
CLASSROOM
COURTYARD
UPPER SHOP
LOWER SHOP
SECTION C through courtyard

03 05

AOC

Synthesizing a participative architecture

AOC, New Architecture Centre, London, England, 2005.

Geoff Shearcroft and Daisy Froud of the firm AOC with Tom Coward and Vincent Lacorvara established their practice together in 2003. Nina Rappaport discussed their work with them in their office in London. They were the Louis I. Kahn Visiting Professors at Yale, teaching an advanced studio in Fall 2011.

Nina Rappaport: How did you realize that you could start a firm together? Geoff Shearcroft: All of us, except for Daisy, are architects who studied at the Royal College of Art [RCA]. Daisy completed a master's degree in cultural memory, having read languages at Cambridge. We started to work together on competitions while teaching at Nottingham University, the Welsh School of Architecture in Cardiff, the Architectural Association, the Bartlett, and then at London Metropolitan University, where we've taught for the past six years.

Daisy Froud: Before setting up AOC, I worked in community-led regeneration to help people change their neighborhoods, and I became increasingly frustrated by the way architects dealt with the information we gave them. Because of our shared interest in the narratives of everyday life, the four of us set up what we called a "loose group" to explore how to make better connections between architectural practice and those narratives.

So often in Europe, there are opportunities for young architects to start small with competitions and then build a firm. It's a way to figure out if you are like-minded and can work together. GS: There was a turning point at the RCA when Tom, Vincent, and I had an intense review without any tutors and realized the potential for a richer conversation when there is an absence of hierarchy and a strong sense of trust. We then became committed to the idea that a collective effort would be a lot better than an individual one.

How does brainstorming become a collective design process? GS: We've explored different ways of designing together, but it works best when it's difficult to tell who did what. The desire to lose individual authorship is an important part of our design process. If the hand of the designer is too evident in the finished building, it can be claustrophobic. We are influenced by James Joyce's approach — as in *Ulysses,* where every chapter uses a different but appropriate style to support the narrative. This approach can be carried through into architecture by developing a process to identify an appropriate style. We always try to work with an open, participatory process that will allow a number of people to contribute.

Would you say this is how your Post-Modernist concepts develop, in terms of cultural identity? DF: We definitely evolved from a Post-Modern consciousness of the world. For me, it comes from literary theory and philosophy — thinking about personal and collective identities and the relationships between self, language, and the world. Established concepts like Barthes' "death of the author" were fundamental to my understanding of, and shaped my approach to, cultural production. In architecture, I realized these ideas to be less commonly accepted, although there was clearly an interesting discussion around how buildings are perceived, and used, so that inhabitants take ownership, rather than the architect. I don't think it's that helpful when the theory is directly applied — that is, overly focusing on "reading" buildings as texts or collections of symbols. But we had many stimulating conversations early on about the minimum an architect can do and what strategic elements need to be there, especially in process, to allow space and diverse human life to continually evolve and find appropriate forms.

What were the first projects that established your thinking as a firm? DF: The first competition we entered was not particularly architectural. It challenged us to think of a way to intervene in shrinking cities. Rather than stress over how to physically transform unused territory, we developed Polyopoly, a board game that functioned as an inverted Monopoly. It allowed us, and others, to explore possible subtle and incremental bottom-up regeneration strategies, with non-professionals playing a meaningful role, and encouraged thinking about the generation of non-monetary forms of value.

Do you ever regret that you've made your work too much fun? As young architects, don't you have to present a more somber front to be taken seriously? DF: Well, yes and no. We're aware that our focus on process and on establishing a productive conversation with potential users — particularly early on, rather than rushing to design a building — may have resulted in us not being taken seriously as architects. Particularly when it comes to the

12 Important ideas about the Lift New Parliament that emerged from the creative workshops
plus another from the sharing/priorities event

1. It should be accessible & inclusive, in the broadest and most creative sense of the term
2. It needs to offer spaces both large and small
3. It needs to change character in each place it goes and take on elements of each place
4. It needs to be flexible and adaptable, with moving elements
5. It needs to have homely qualities about it: to be cosy, warm & intimate as well as a public space
6. It needs to spill out and leak into the wider environment ... have fuzzy boundaries, whilst being safe & secure
7. Eating is really important (but so is the smell)
8. It needs windows - light, particularly day light is really important
9. It needs to have many different entrances and ways in
10. It needs to allow people on the outside to have a sense of what happens on the inside
11. It needs to be easy to navigate and well signposted (but with a sense of adventure)
12. It needs to offer different levels & height

PLUS...

13. It needs to be eco-friendly and responsibly limit its impact on the environment

AOC, Spatial constitution for The Lift, a demountable performace and meeting space for the London International Festival of Theatre, 2008.

"beauty parade" of competitions, we've often been reluctant to reduce a scheme to a couple of winning images. But we are very serious, and very rigorous, about generating a good brief. When we enter competitions, we spend a lot of time understanding the contexts and cultures from which a built form will ultimately emerge. But it seems crazy to fix a form to this before you actually work with the client and those involved. And that's been problematic at times but less so now, when people hire us precisely because of that focus.

GS: The seriousness thing is interesting — how can we overcome perceptions of it? One way is to be involved in things outside of our practice. Vincent, for example, also works within a planning department in one of London's boroughs, commissioning projects, developing planning policy, working on master plans, and negotiating schemes with major developers.

DF: And I used to train local politicians in understanding and critiquing design for London's architecture center, Open City. It is important for council members to feel confident about what good design is before they become involved in exercising power over the built environment, such as through planning committees. We aimed to give them the skills to argue for considered design and against mediocrity.

GS: As we have begun to make buildings at an increasing scale and complexity, I hope people are realizing the serious intent behind our apparent play. In 2011, we completed Spa School, a new building for children who are high on the autistic spectrum. It continues our exploration of the relationship between iconography and weightiness, of image and experience, of critique and construction, of suggested and prescribed uses. But, more fundamentally, it is on budget, on time, and exceeds the users' expectations.

How do you engage the client or community in the design process? Do you worry about a project not following your design aesthetic when you leave it to the client to fill in the blanks? DF: In short, no! A space needs to be non-precious enough to take on its own life after we leave. We focus on developing good briefs with people and then working with users through creative exploration to make good decisions, in a clear and accountable way, in response. This often involves challenging initial assumptions, ours and the client's. But, ultimately, it is still our job, as architects, to find a built or spatialized form as an outcome of those conversations and exercises. It's not about evacuating the architect from the process but about, to quote Jeremy Till quoting John Forester, "making sense together." Our aim with the physical output is not to leave "blanks." We strongly believe that the spaces that give you the most freedom as a user are not empty "white" ones — where, theoretically, anything is possible but, in reality, little of interest happens — but those that offer you suggestive elements to respond to in your own way as a user. That's the challenge: to define the space enough to provide subtle suggestion and positive provocation, but not prescription. And to allow that space to continue to evolve once we have gone.

Often, architects don't even know their constituents or how to engage a community in meaningful and constructive ways as an aspect of design. DF: Yes. Or the engagement is reduced to whipping out your completed design, sticking it up and asking, "What do you think?" Or — my most disliked phrase — "Have your say!"

GS: Historically, there's been quite a disjunction between architects who are interested in engaging people and those who are interested primarily in form. We're interested in putting the two together. I think Polyopoly allowed us to create a visually strong object that allowed a participative process to happen through the act of playing a board game, transforming the board aesthetically, spatially, and socially in the process.

But the design component is not just a game. I saw it exhibited at the 2008 Venice Biennale, in the "Experimental Architecture" section of the Italian Pavilion. GS: In that reworked version we explored the notion of interaction in an exhibition format. People could visit the first six stops along the board and were encouraged to explore various futures for Venice, rather than the original site: a suburb of Liverpool.

DF: Our early projects have in common the desire to create spaces of possibility, physical and notional "suggestive spaces." In 2005, we entered a competition for a new building for London's Architecture Foundation. Zaha Hadid won, and we came in third, but there was so much press that we used it as an opportunity to establish ourselves. While Polyopoly explored the idea of the board as a fertile space where different encounters can happen, our Architecture Foundation concept was that of a building that sets up various possibilities of use and makes possible multiple spatial encounters between different users.

GS: We played off the fact that the competition happened just before Christmas and made our presentation board in the form of a fully functional Advent calendar.

This narrative aspect of your work is especially potent in presentations. How did you begin that? It's a very Pop or Post-Modern attitude that engages the public. GS: One reason we established an architectural practice with an interpreter as a founder was because we hoped to improve the relationship between the brief and the realized building. Drawings are a key tool for interpretation, but the drawing must be appropriate to the individuals involved. We sample drawing techniques from artists, illustrators, directors, architects — whatever seems to work best for communicating with the intended viewers. For many projects, we develop a spatial constitution — a drawn brief — that provides a stepping-stone between the user's needs and our architectural designs. One of the first public projects we developed this for was the Lift, a demountable performance and meeting space for the London International Festival of Theatre. The spatial constitution was an essential device for developing a brief with ten separate community groups, all located in the Olympic boroughs, but it also provided a useful tool for checking the design development against the original intentions, allowing a greater level of accountability between architects and the client and its end users.

Did this method ever create problems when presenting your ideas to the architecture and design community, especially because of the emphasis on narrative rather than architecture with a capital A? Maybe that is part of your critique, along with the work of firms such as FAT or MUF. GS: Much of our work has been dismissed by other architects as "collage-like," but we have been attempting to create buildings that translate the looseness of our collages into realized buildings. One of our first projects, the Janet Summers Early Years Centre, is a collage of found elements, adapted ready-mades, coded surfaces, and new materials that seems to invite the same level of interaction and misuse by the users that our drawings and models do. On a larger scale, for *Walk in the Olympic Park* at London 2012, we curated a route through the waterways and parklands that told the story of the park's transformation through artworks and pavilions by different artists and designers with a narrative overlay and installations made from reused, reconfigured red telephone boxes by us.

How and why are graphics important in your work? GS: The relationship between the graphic, which can be associated with Pop, and the materiality of architecture is something we continue to explore — it goes back to the tension in Post-Modernism between surface and materiality. At St. Saviour's and St. Olave's School, we have used graphic elements in a variety of ways, each appropriate to its context. On the building's public entrance we have applied vinyl supersized graphics to a taut curtain wall that acts as a three-story information billboard to visitors but as an abstract, delicate privacy screen for those on the inside. On the west elevation, facing a busy highway, eight-foot-high, precast-concrete letters create a civic monumentality that announces the previously discrete school to those driving by. Internally, pattern and color are introduced on all surfaces to suggest potential uses.

What types of public-realm projects are you working on, and how do you use ideas about civic engagement and participation when designing the public sphere? DF: For the past two years, we've been developing a new community center and housing and public space in Nunhead, in south London. The housing came first. It's on council-owned land in an area where people feel housing is being crammed into every available space, and they wanted the site for community allotments. But the council is required to hit housing targets and make efficient use of public assets. Over eighteen months, we ran a careful, committed process in which, through a series of workshops and public events involving hundreds of people, we gradually designed a scheme that was acceptable to them.

We were honest throughout the process about which decisions the people could influence, carefully explaining national, regional, and local planning policy, and encouraging them to focus energy on areas

AOC, Janet Summers Early Years Centre, London, England, 2006.

about which, within the scope of our brief, we could listen and they could make a difference. If they still wanted to protest, we encouraged them to do that through the planning applications process or even activism. However, our focus was on establishing a metaphorical project space in which we engaged with people creatively and respectfully as intelligent human beings, and we learned from them about the character of their area. Over time, we found our way to a scheme that we are proud of as architects, and yet it differs significantly from our initial proposals — and that has been very much shaped by debate. Considerable energy was invested in preparing graphics, texts, and questions that assumed no professional knowledge while supporting a productive conversation about complex issues. And we continually fed back changes to the local community, explaining what we had done and why.

As a result of the trust built, we were asked to design an adjacent community center with a local group. This project has involved an intensive participatory design process, run in parallel with the group's business-plan development, with the task as much about developing social and economic structures as physical ones. We also have recently started re-landscaping the adjacent park — again, developing a clear brief and set of priorities with local residents and businesses.

People also care more about something if they're a part of the process, rather than having something imposed upon them. DF: I think, over time, experience has proven that a belief in drawing on wider community intelligence was not merely the conviction of naïve young optimists but a productive methodology — time and time again, people really engage and provide well-reasoned responses.

Synthesizing a participative architecture

AOC are Post-Modern architects. By this, we do not mean that we employ a Post-Modern style, although we are certainly interested in the possibilities of architecture that make inventive use of visual and spatial references to explore — or playfully subvert — shared meaning. We mean that we are conscious of operating in a world in which social and political structures are continually called into question, beliefs and memories are slippery things, and space is not an inert backdrop, but a live site of meaning production — space is a cultural practice.

Our task as architects is to help needs, desires, processes, and narratives find form — sometimes provisional, sometimes more enduring — while remaining conscious that these forms will always be as imperfect and contradictory as the practices they host and reflect. We may have, and indeed wish to have, little control over what happens. But we can help create the conditions in which, if the political will is there, productive things can happen, some of which will be unforeseen, unpredictable, or just positively curious.

Driven by a desire within the limited power afforded to architects to generate environments that support aspirations toward a more participative democracy, we are drawn to complex projects with multiple stakeholders — housing, mixed-use, master plans, cultural institutions, public-private partnerships. Here, our approach to the politics is as important as that taken to the design. Or rather, here, design is politics. Likewise, our studio briefs tend to have, at their heart, the exploration of networks of relationships. We encourage students to enjoy, and engage with, the complexity of social institutions and with the individuals, groups, and objects that constitute them. And to think about how space can respond to these things.

Our Yale studio was no exception. The task was to design public-access storage, in the suburbs of a U.K. town, to house the vast collection of a famous British cultural institution. At one level, this is obviously a functional challenge: to house X cubic meters of artifacts in a way that they can be easily viewed and even handled. At another level, it is an aesthetic challenge: to find an appropriate visual form and brand for an institution.

But equally important was the philosophical investigation — conducted both at the scale of the individual's relation to the artifact and at that of the building's to the public realm — into the nature and role of these traditionally top-down bodies in the twenty-first century. Inherited assumptions about value were given a good shakedown: for example, the value of suburban space versus urban, of "commercial" building typologies versus respectable "architectural" ones, and of a referential architectural language versus a "pure" one. Then, the possible social and formal relationships that might emerge from this questioning position became the source of design development.

OUR STARTING POINT: A CONTEMPORARY PUBLIC REPOSITORY

A Post-Modern democratic society — in which everyone's past and every narrative are deemed of potential value and thus may arguably be recorded and stored — requires an appropriate container, a new typology, in which to hoard. What form might this take?

Museum scholar Elaine Gurian makes a provocative proposal for the museum's evolving role in democratic society in her influential 2006 article "The Essential Museum." Her vision is of the institution as a participative and social experience in which visitors can directly engage with the majority of a collection's artifacts. "If the public wants access to things, then it stands to reason that museums should provide access to lots of things. In fact, why not set up a visual investigation of all, or almost all of, what the museum holds?" To be welcoming, this new visible storage and knowledge system needs, Gurian emphasizes, to be coupled with responsive space design. She suggests that, in particular, the shopping mall might be learned from because its spatial structures permit informal "lurking" and browsing and, importantly, facilitate direct contact and an intimate relationship between visitor and artifact.

This argument is interesting when considered alongside trends in collection storage. Despite increased digitization, the perceived homogeneity of globalization has led to renewed emphasis on the "authenticity" of material artifacts, with a subsequent increased demand for "hard" storage. Thus, institutions are expanding their collections beyond the crumbling confines of predominantly urban mansions into generic warehouses in post-suburban towns. Oxford's Bodleian Library, for example, home to not one but four copies of the Magna Carta and historically housed in an eclectic mix of buildings around the City of Dreaming Spires, recently declared its shelves "one hundred and thirty percent full." The solution? A new, 127,000-square-foot book repository in a steel shed on an industrial estate in Swindon, a seemingly non-descript nearby town, eighty miles west of London. However, while such public repositories may provide safe, controlled storage, they offer negligible access to collections and little contribution to the peripheral sites they colonize.

Drawing synthesizing Stirling's Clore Gallery at Tate Britain, Tony Craigg's *Cumulus* and the New Haven Ikea Store.

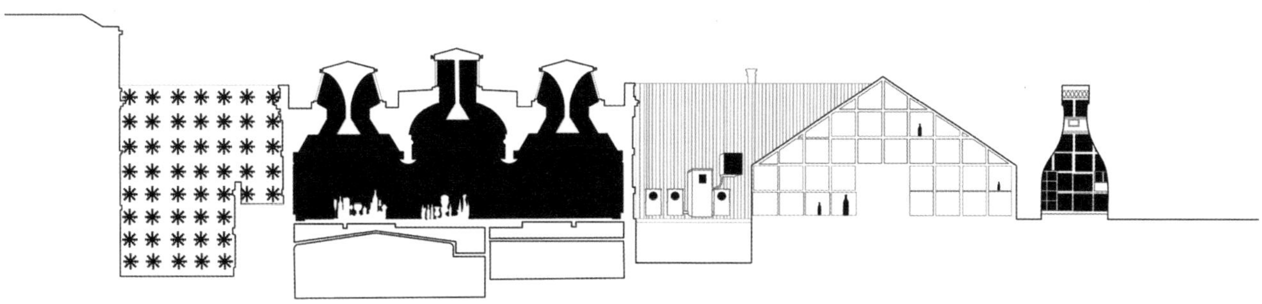

Our studio takes these two conditions — a spatial phenomenon, born largely of economic necessity, and a cultural aspiration — and asks how they might inform each other. How might architecture support a different relationship between viewer, artifact, and institution, taking advantage of the potential "freedoms" — both of space and from convention — of a suburban site and of a less "precious" building typology?

BIG-BOX INSTITUTIONS IN A POST-SUBURBAN WORLD

> "For me, the most visionary architect, the one who best understood the ineluctable disorder in which we live, remains Frank Lloyd Wright and his Broadacre City. . . . The projects I have been working on have been situated in a territory that can no longer be called suburbia but must be referred to as the borders, or limits, of the periphery. The contemporary city, the one composed of these peripheries, ought to yield a sort of manifesto, a premature homage to a form of modernity, which, when compared to cities of the past, might seem devoid of possibilities, but in which we will one day recognize as many gains as losses."
> — Rem Koolhaas, "Toward the Contemporary City" (1989)

Early twentieth-century Modern architecture appropriated the commercial and industrial vernacular of its time — grain silos and concrete sheds — to establish a new and relevant architecture. Similarly, we believe today's practice needs to embrace the communicative impact and construction technologies of the contemporary vernacular. An increasingly constant presence in the postwar landscape, the suburban "big box" has enjoyed a flurry of interest in the past decade. Villainized as a symbol of all that is wrong with the American dream, it continues to evolve toward ever-greater efficiencies.

In the U.K., the post-suburban city, which is the dominant urban form of developed nations, houses many big boxes. Millions of citizens spend leisure time visiting the retail warehouses of brands such as IKEA and Homebase (the British Home Depot). Typologically similar, yet programmatically distinct, to the new models of institutional storage, these outlets offer an internal landscape of pallet towers from which consumers select and purchase symbolic capital in artifact form. Our studio chose to explore how a group of established public repositories — the V&A Museum, the Tate Gallery, the British Museum, the British Library, the Royal Armouries — might learn from this popular cultural activity through a process of re-sampling the box that accommodates it: the forms, scale, technologies, and associations. What new relationship between artifacts and viewers might this encourage? What new audiences might it reach?

Building on Frank Lloyd Wright's thesis of the urban periphery as fertile ground for the architectural realization of democracy, we chose Swindon as our site of inquiry. At first glance, it may appear to be a typical hinterland town: a declining post-industrial center encircled by housing, retail, and industrial estates, all loosely embraced by a ring road. However, further research reveals that its gross value-added per capita is higher than that of London's, that it was the first U.K. town to provide free broadband service for all citizens, that it has the nation's most cinema seats per capita, and that, in 2010, it was "twinned" with Disneyland. In short, it is a sprawling, value-adding manufacturing node, hard-wired to global communications and media networks — the post-suburban city par excellence.

While this "sprawl" may lack the density, heritage, and cultural baggage of its urban neighbors, or perhaps because of this lack, it offered interesting spatial opportunities for our project. We asked, rather than keep our collective memories in cramped, huddled conditions, reinforcing retrogressive impressions of the guardian institutions, why not move them out to the edge where they have space to breathe, adapt, and be productive?

We worked closely with the local council to identify a selection of sites for new public repositories, initiating a useful discussion about the potential civic value of such development. With the National Trust, the U.K.'s most significant heritage charity, having shifted its headquarters from London to Swindon in 2005, politicians and planners were keen to explore the possibility of similar institutional investment. This genuine political interest was important to us in terms of legitimizing the task we set for our students: it was evident that our project was not merely the stuff of academic fantasy or architectural whimsy.

SAMPLING A "NEW CIVIC"

> "The mind of the mature poet differs from that of the immature one not precisely in any valuation of 'personality,' not being necessarily more interesting, or having 'more to say,' but rather by being a more finely perfected medium in which special, or very varied, feelings are at liberty to enter into new combinations.
> — T. S. Eliot (*The Sacred Wood*, 1920)

AOC has always been drawn to an architectural tradition of sampling and synthesizing: selecting spatial and symbolic elements from our surroundings and recombining these in new and, at times, surprising yet always resolved and coherent ways. Soane, Lutyens, Venturi, and Stirling are valued forebears here. We have also looked to other disciplines to help us consider the what, how, and why of this method, not only for generating formal proposals but also for supporting ongoing inhabitation and use.

In *Post-Production: Culture as Screenplay: How Art Reprograms the World* (2002), for example, curator Nicolas Bourriaud outlines a significant recent shift in cultural production, saying, "The democratization of computers and the appearance of sampling allowed for the emergence of a new cultural configuration, whose emblematic figures are the programmer and the producer. The remixer has become more important than the instrumentalist, the rave more exciting than the concert." A musical culture of re-configuration, co-production, and collaboration suggests a new role for the artist and a different kind of creation, with useful parallels for architecture. Perhaps the architect should identify more with the DJ-producer than with the singer-songwriter in the sense that architects, too, are carefully selecting existing elements and synthesizing them into new, considered combinations. What if his or her focus was on creating a cultural space in which a public can participate and to which it can contribute?

Sampling, whatever the discipline, is a mode of engagement with an existing world — a world that is familiar, that has been experienced, and that defines our memories. Our studio focused on how this mode of production might help generate a more popular and participatory architecture. With few direct architectural precedents to inform the design of an open-access repository, our approach was to sample elements from both the institutions themselves and their new post-suburban sites. In doing so, we opened up opportunities for the new proposals to be familiar and relevant, tapping into, and engaging with, cultural memory.

METHODOLOGY

1 PROTOTYPE: The Big-Box Institution (three weeks)

In pairs, students analyzed the architecture and identity of one of five British institutions: the British Library, the British Museum, the Royal Armouries, the Tate and the Victoria & Albert Museum.

Large-scale section study of light storage at IKEA. The drawing illustrates the strata of product display, demonstration, and storage.

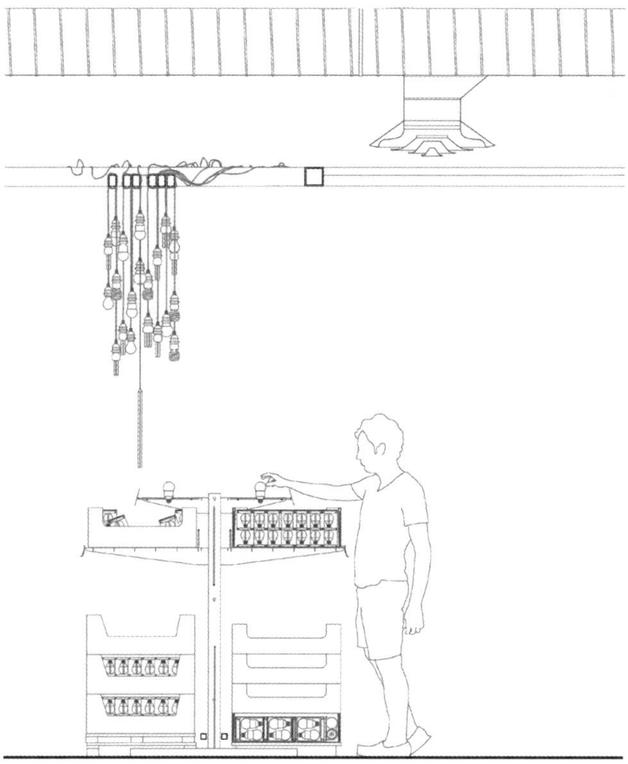

They selected and sampled three elements: one or more architectural elements of the institution, an object from its collection, and the architecture of a typical New Haven big-box. These found elements were synthesized into digital and physical models and became the basis for a studio lexicon of sampling and synthesizing, provoking reflection on the relationships between visual image and experienced object.

Each institution has its own spatial identity that influences the way in which its collection is experienced. The collection artifacts also have their own unique formal qualities that are loaded with associations. Sampling these from afar becomes a purely formal act, inspired by visual response. We embraced the limitations of this technique, honing our visual sensibilities upon the sampled shapes to understand the significance of their forms and think about what we were instinctively drawn to and why.

Synthesizing the students' chosen elements with the found typologies of the local post-suburban city then initiated discussions about the ways in which sampling might inform a more overtly architectural response appropriate to our study area.

2 BRIEF: Sampling an Encounter (three weeks, including field trip to the project site)

In new pairs, students immersed themselves in one of five Swindon sites using both qualitative and quantitative analysis to produce a 1:500 scale model, the basis for future proposals.

A visit to London allowed students to form relationships with their assigned institutions, meeting curators and undertaking both detached observation of, and immersive engagement in, their building and its collection. We also visited a number of existing repositories, from the Soane Museum and Strawberry Hill to the Natural History Museum's dinosaur hall to Alsop's Peckham Library, with its distinctive book-stacks-on-sticks structure. Traveling west, we compared Oxford, the medieval city-as-repository, with Swindon, its post-suburban upstart, visiting Bodleian book storage, old and new. Swindon's Urban Design Team then introduced us to the physical realities, histories, and potentials of the five sites.

Throughout, we continued to consider what to sample and how to synthesize, generating a broad source book as well as design methodologies with which to initiate proposals upon our return. Back at Yale, students developed a brief for their institution's new repository. Their starting point was an observed 1:12 scale detail of an encounter between a visitor and an artifact; this exercise was designed to provoke thinking about the actual ways in which an individual engages, and might desire to engage, an object in space. This detail was then used as a starting point for design, rethinking and remaking the institution from the inside out. Donlyn Lyndon, in the seminal essay "Toward Making Places" (1962), suggests that a key dynamic in the shift from providing formal objects to creating inhabitable places is to " 'let in' the user, not as a hapless occupant filling a chair in the 'living room' or 'giving scale' to the elevation but as an active participant. . . . The user must be allowed to participate, to reclaim through his acts that which has been abstracted from him." This task was a practical way of considering that dynamic.

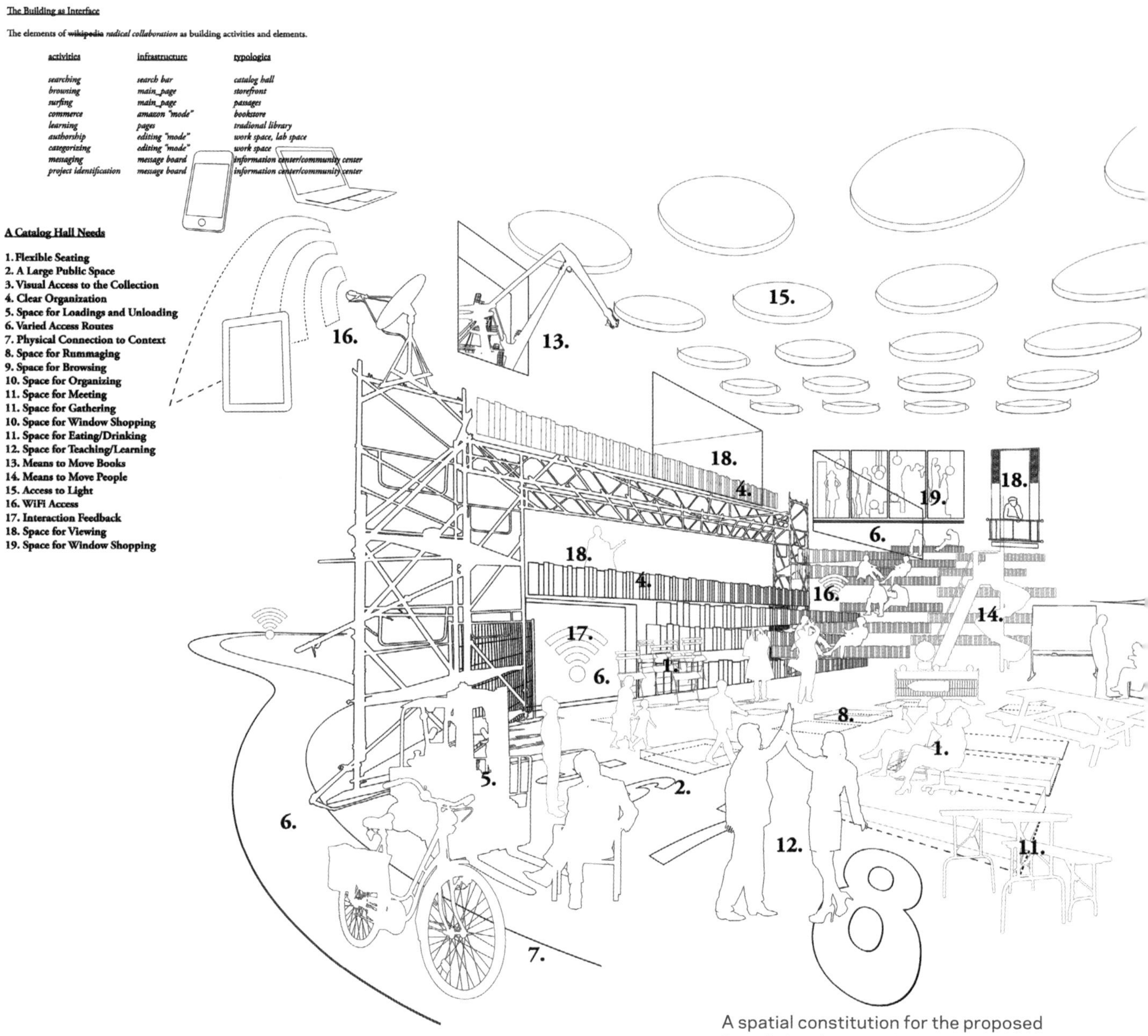

A spatial constitution for the proposed British Cataloguing Centre.

3 PROPOSAL: A Contemporary Public Repository (seven weeks)

Each student then developed a design for a new public repository for their institution on their Swindon site. The design development focused on the relationship between the institution and the (sub)urban site, using physical models; the image of the building itself, through large-format color images that were constructed, not rendered; and the relationship between use and construction, through scaled, detailed drawings. The outcome of this activity were buildings redolent of both the old institution and its new neighborhood, the historical artifacts and their new big-box vessel (a historical artifact in itself), and the embedded inherited culture of the historical collections and their new cultural context of enhanced engagement. Familiar forms were subverted, resulting in a formal evolution that was both slight and radical. Stepping beyond the limitations of abstract contemporary expression and playfully embracing associations with the past, we sought to create appropriate forms and communicative façades, that were infused with useful details, nurturing an informed combination of form and use and fostering productive relationships among visitor, artifact, and place.

Studio Work

01 SAMPLING EXPERIENCES

For many, the enduring aspect of a collection, beyond the actual objects, is the character of its arrangement in a set of specific spaces. The relationship between an institution and its architecture is often implicit. Therefore, students were encouraged to understand the ways in which the collection was displayed, stored, conserved, and discussed as an expression of the institution and its relationship with the public. Experiential qualities themselves became a provocation — conceptual, retinal, environmental, or societal, for example — toward a proposition. Proposals sampled existing architectures and synthesized them to create new combinations of familiar spatial experiences. It was often found that sampled qualities taken from a city resonated at different frequencies in a post-suburban place.

CHRISTOS BOLOS
TATE AS COUNTRY HOUSE

This project situates a publicly accessible repository for the Tate Collection, in Swindon, by hybridizing a big-box storage warehouse with the British countryhouse typology. First, this branch of the Tate uses Swindon's advantageous central location between the four existing Tate galleries. The Tate Swindon would absorb all the Tate's undisplayed objects, which compromise the majority of the collection, and provide ample room for the ever-expanding collection. In this role, the Tate Swindon would become the central distribution center for the Tate collection. Second, in re-instituting the "dining room" as the center of social life and as the primary venue for viewing art, the Tate Swindon democratizes the country house by allowing individuals and groups to hold events as well as curate the art that surrounds them while they dine.

01 01

To further make the Tate Swindon an integral part of the Tate's operations, a cue was taken from the Tate Store, which is the building that houses the Tate's undisplayed objects and currently functions as a staging venue for new acquisi-

01 02

01 03

01 04

01 05

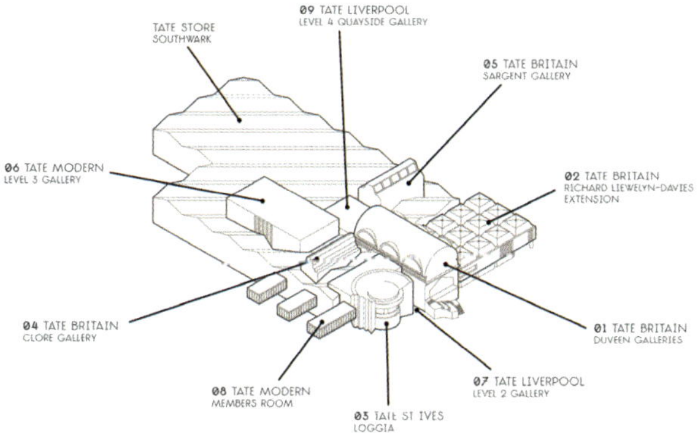

01.01 Relative location to Tate galleries and storage.

01.02 Approach, south façade.

01.03 Concept image: big-box storage warehouse combined with a British country house.

01.04 Final entrance charrette model.

01.05 Tate "sampled" galleries diagram.

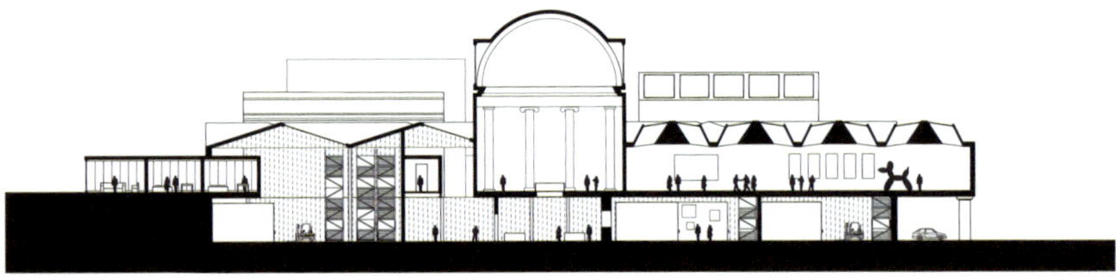

01 06

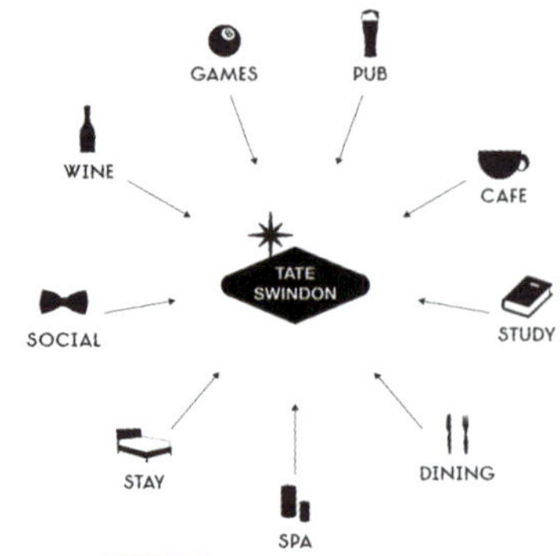

01 07

01 08

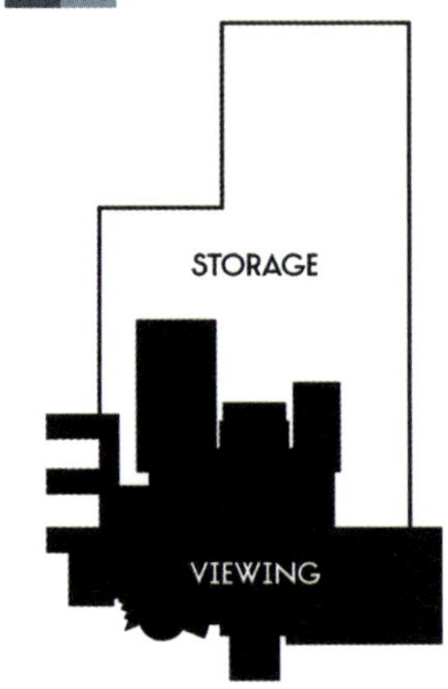

01 09

tions or upcoming exhibits. Currently, a mock gallery must be constructed and subsequently torn down every three months to "test" the various artworks under museum conditions. The Tate Swindon improves up on this model, making it more accurate and experientially rich by directly reconstructing various rooms from the existing four Tates. This set up provides an array of spaces in which the collection can be rehearsed. Although these rooms are infused with new programs such as overnight rooms and study areas for scholars, they are exact replicas of their original counterparts, thereby allowing staff to test artwork against the conditions of any Tate prior to transporting a piece.

The rooms within the Tate Swindon are arranged in a manner both emblematic of traditional country house planning and respectful of the building's newly infused programmatic functions. The country house portion of the scheme is oriented toward the picturesque — and, in the future, possibly suburban — southern side of the site, while the storage shed fronts the A419 highway, to facilitate the distribution operations of the facility. The two parts, country house and warehouse, then come together to provide users access to the vast storage space from the intimate gallery areas. This strategy allows for public access to the often-unexhibited objects of the Tate Collection, allowing users to sift through storage racks of, say, paintings and gain a unique experience. Thus, the domestic and the curated is contrasted with the industrial and impromptu.

01.06 Sections of Tate Swindon.

01.07 Program strategy diagram.

01.08 Final model.

01.09 Program diagram.

STEPHEN GAGE

THE BRITISH LIBRARY: THE SWINDON SOUND & MEDIA ARCHIVE

The British Library, the national library of the United Kingdom, was created in 1973 to consolidate several of the country's most important collections. With over 150 million items and growing by over three million items each year, the British Library is one of the largest and most diverse collections in the world. Current long-term plans for removing most of the collection to inaccessible, off-site storage in Yorkshire conflict with the library's mission of giving unprecedented access to its collections. Furthermore, many of the library's smaller collections remain unknown and underused despite unparalleled richness of content.

This proposal calls for a new, long-term vision based on strategic regional centers for different portions of the collection. Located on the National Rail network in post-industrial hinterland cities with cheap land and building costs, these new regional centers store the smaller collections, relieving storage pressure at the main St. Pancras site and providing the necessary viewing equipment the overcrowded London site cannot.

The Swindon Sound & Media Archive serves as a prototype for this new type of regional library, combining the sound archive, printed music, and various performance programs. This unique collection includes over four million audio, video, and printed music media, ranging from popular and classical music to wildlife sounds and rare performance recordings. With the Swindon Sound & Media Archive, there is an opportunity to link the storage itself with the mechanism for using the collection. Through this link, multiple audiences are engaged at multiple scales of experience, from local residents to research specialists. In the process, a dialogue emerges between intimacy and monumentality. The vast scale and repetitive modules of the collection contrast with the spaces for intimate, personal audio experiences.

After careful analysis of existing needs and future growth, the proposed program is approximately half storage, one quarter viewing and performance, and one quarter support. A central aisle binds together the interior, creating a processional route that weaves through the storage stacks. Interspersed are the viewing and performance spaces, the true public focus of the building. These spaces include a range of scales: larger, public ones for study, performance, theater, a dance club, and an existing McDonald's; and smaller, private ones for recording studios, group nooks, and individual audio booths. Together, they allow the collection to be experienced in new ways, reaching out to a broader public audience and providing the public with opportunities to mix different parts of the collection.

Architecturally, a structural grid sets up the basic framework in a rhythm that echoes the existing housing to the north of the site. This grid is filled with rows of storage that are organized by media type, resulting in a variable grain and density. These unique and diverse storage rooms reference a diverse set of precedents, some of them directly sampled into the design. Multiple entrances along a public promenade create a vibrant public space that accentuates existing pedestrian routes across the site, connecting downtown Swindon and the train station with the Gorse Hill commercial district.

02 01

02.01 Midterm study collage of possible overlapping functions within the proposed program.

02 02

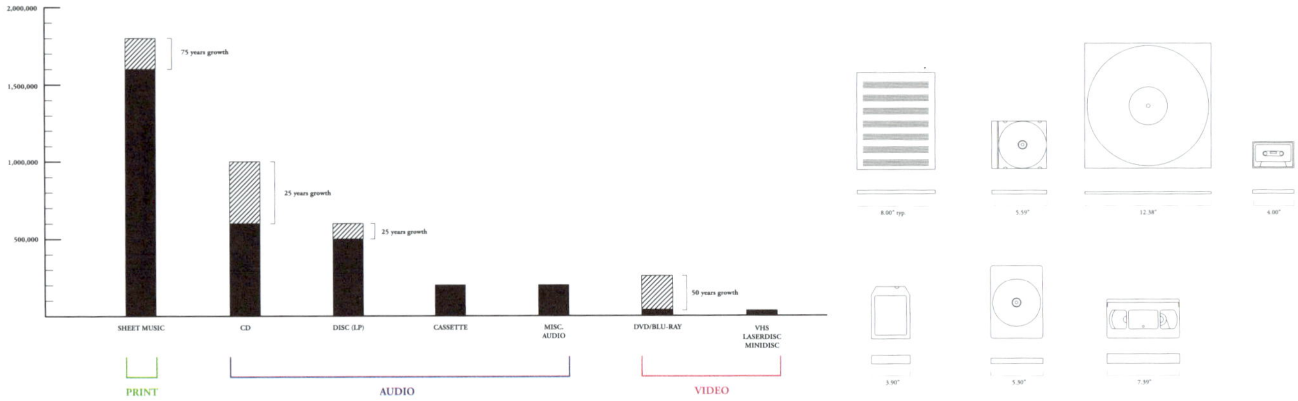

02 03

Materially, the building is composed of a pattern of bricks that form letters of the alphabet based on the existing entry gate at the British Library, St. Pancras. The brick pattern is interwoven with metal siding to form monitors for the warehouse, establishing a dichotomy that speaks to the interaction of the highly specific viewing spaces and repetitive stack and room-storage system. The letters abstractly recall the ordered, systematic nature of the collection, reference the nature of institutional identity in their signage and materiality, and create a dematerialized screen that allows for modulation of light and views into the building.

In the interplay between repetitive storage and highly specific viewing spaces, between clip-on, IKEA-like sheds and warm, human-scaled brick, the project explores the oscillation between the generic and the specific, the monumental and the intimate — oppositions inherent to the uniquely contemporary intersection of large-scale storage with the preservation of cultural heritage.

02.02 The approach: Great Western Way.

02.03 A breakdown of the British Library's media collection based on media type and quantity.

02.04 Initial entrance study model.

02.05 View of the study-space void, with storage beyond.

02.06 Ground floor plan.

02 04

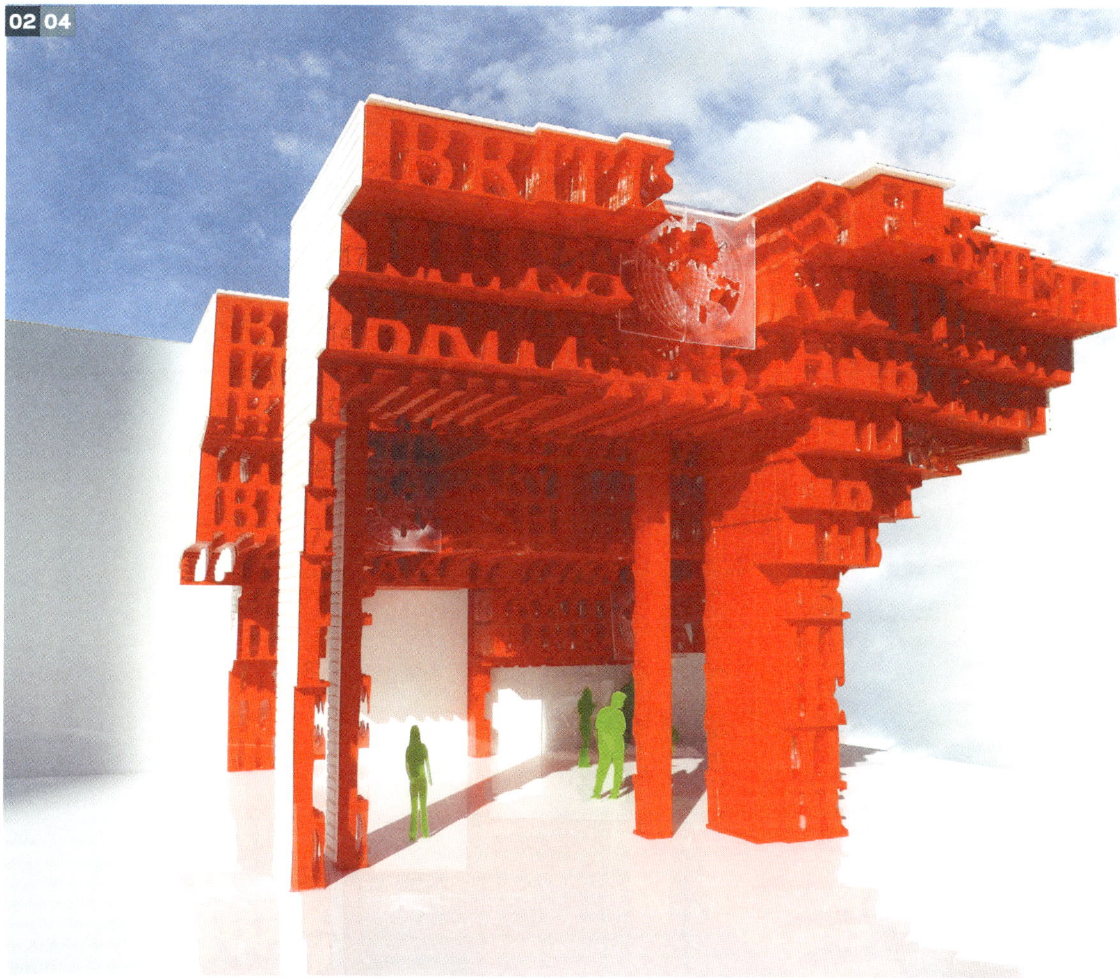

02 05

02 06

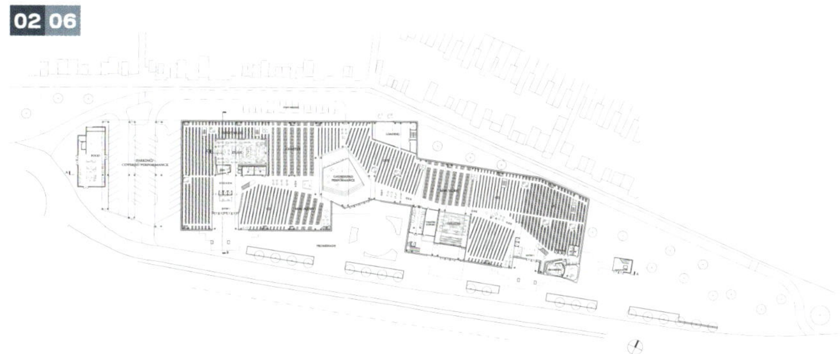

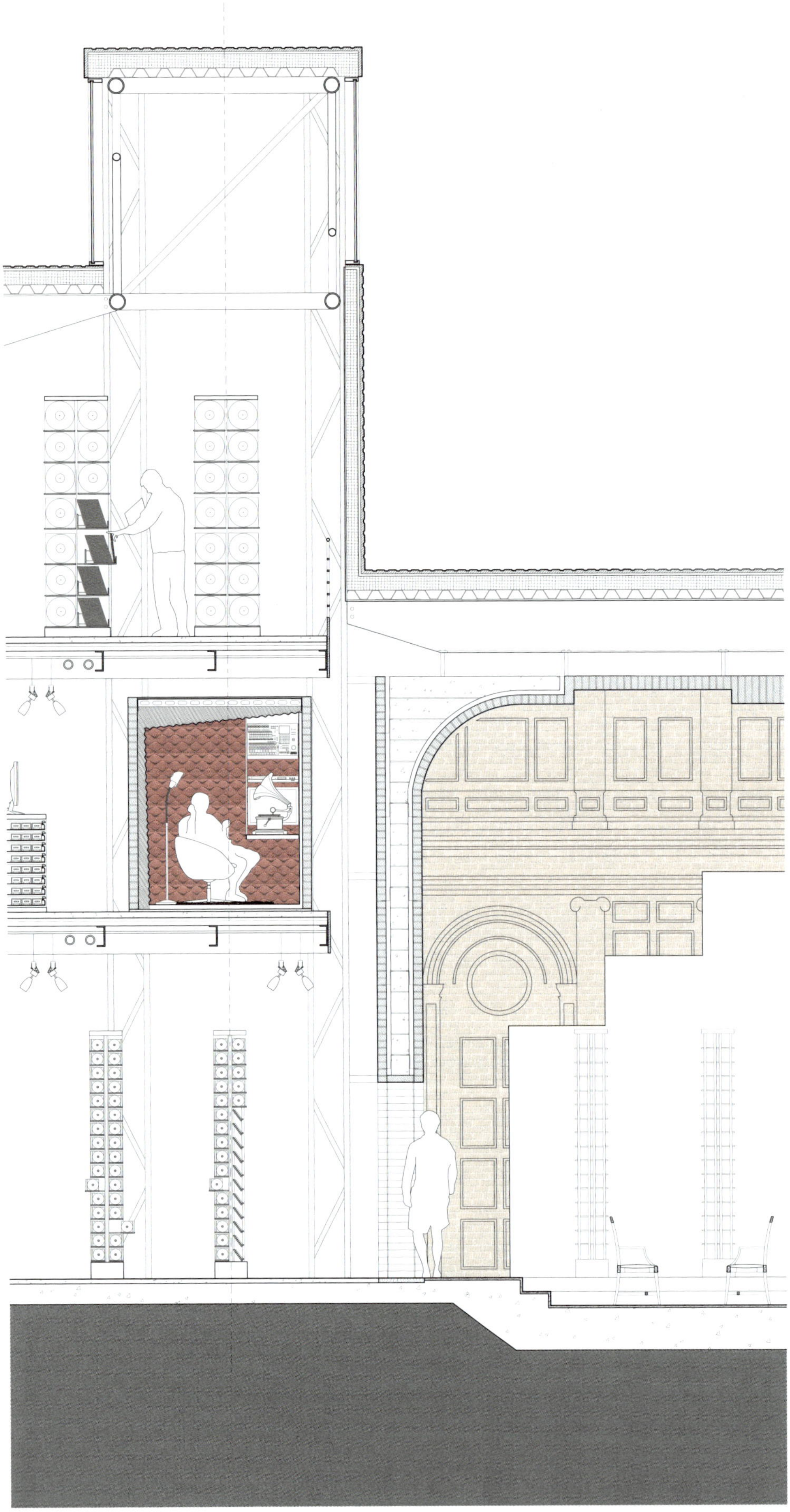

02.07 Detail section at 1:12 scale illustrating the intersection of the study space and storage.

02.08 An axonometric showing the exterior form with the key performance voids pulled out as interior views.

02.09 Renderings of the main elevation showing basic façade modules (top), the brick pattern (middle), and a rendered view (bottom).

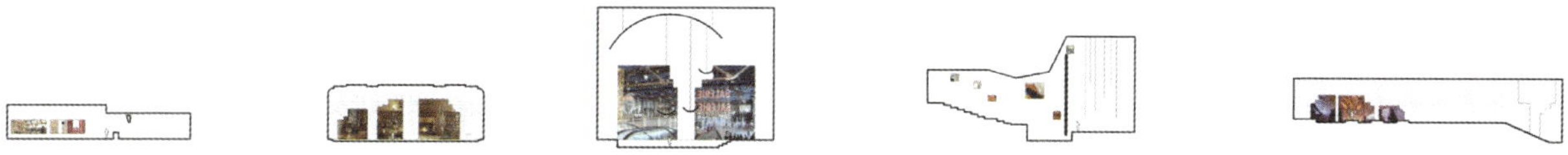
McDonalds
Study
Informal gathering / performance
Theatre
Dance club / lounge

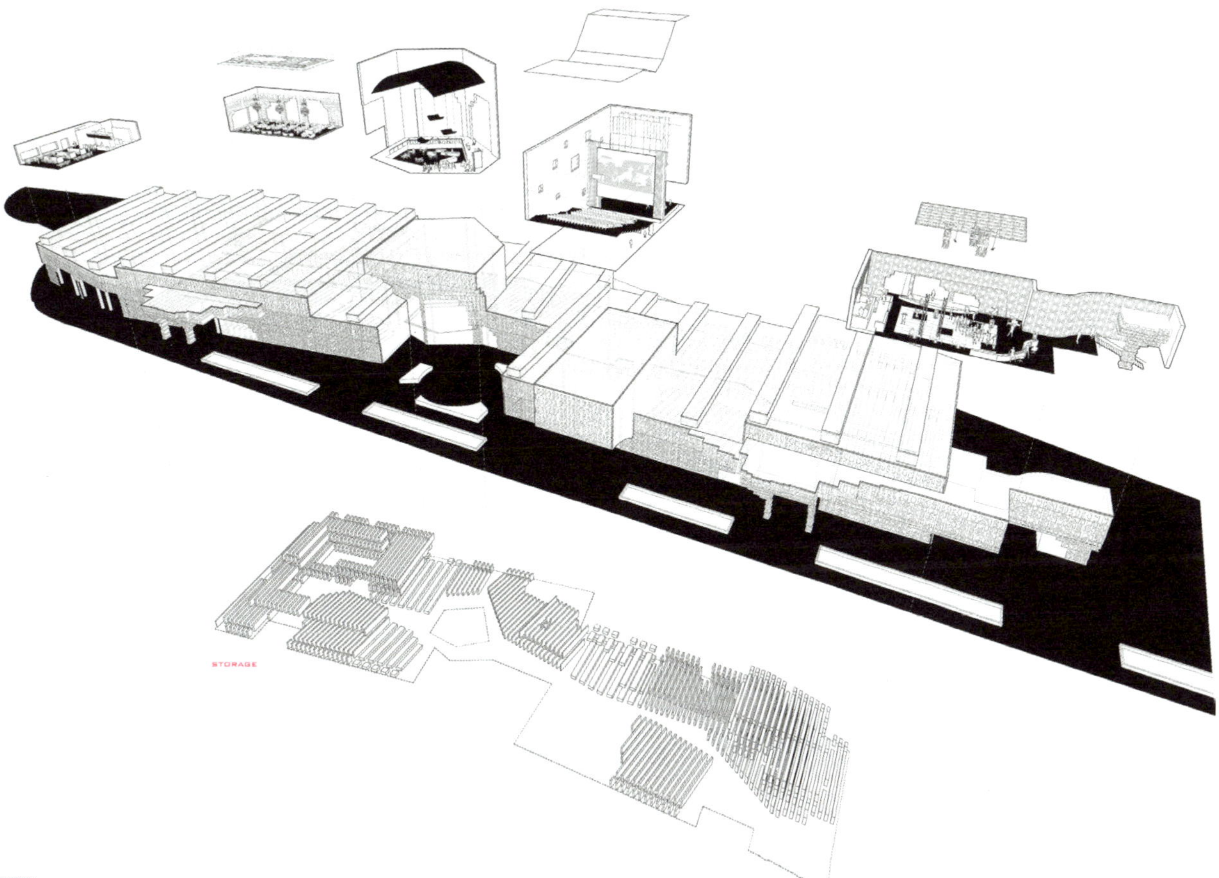
STORAGE

02 08

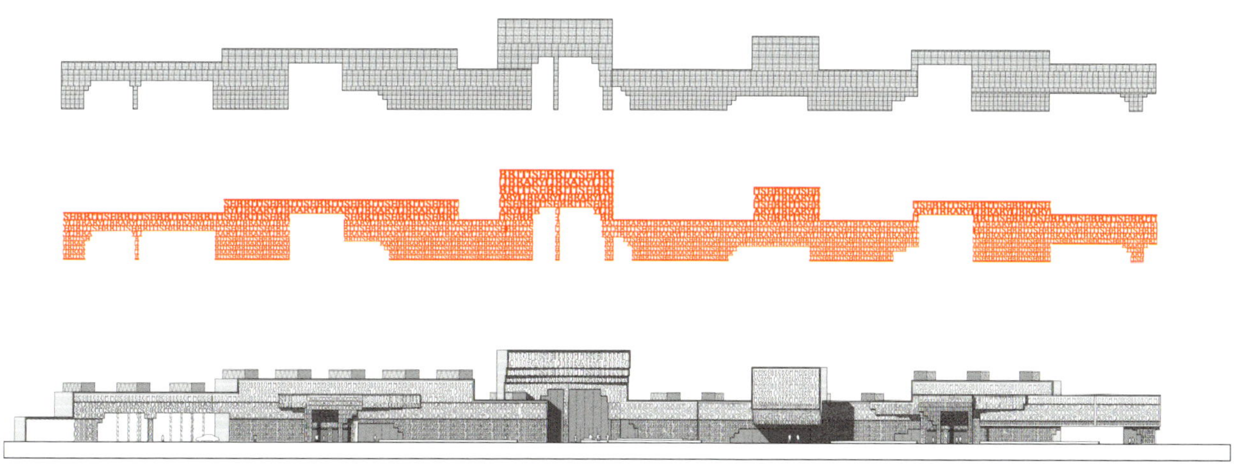

02 09

03 01

JOHN TAYLOR BACHMAN

ROYAL ARMOURIES

The British Royal Armouries currently has a total of 79,000 items in its collection of armor, weapons, art, and a vast number of firearms in its National Firearms Centre. However, there are now only four locations where small parts of the collection are exhibited; approximately only twenty percent of the entire collection can be displayed at any given time, leaving the remaining eighty percent locked away in storage.

On our trip, we were granted special access to the storage facility of the Royal Armouries, in Leeds, England. We visited three levels of storage where we were surrounded by aisle after aisle of spears, swords, and other types of arms and armor. The sheer volume of the collection and its system of organization, which organizes thousands of items into vast arrays, was every bit as impressive as any of the curated displays, yet it remains inaccessible to the public. The goal of the project is to relocate the objects now locked away in Leeds to a new public storage facility in Swindon, ultimately allowing everyone access to one hundred percent of the collection.

The new public storage facility for the British Royal Armouries is proposed for the site of an existing Toys 'R' Us, in Swindon. This site is also the starting point for a planned 10,000-home suburban development. The main challenge of this project was to decide how to appropriately place a warehouse full of functional weapons

03.01 Rendering perspective showing the cul-de-sac of faux-houses on the roof.

03.02 Rendering of the interior showing one of the skylights and how the collection might be displayed.

and ammunition into a suburban neighborhood. The most sensitive, logical, and appropriate solution became camouflage.

One method of applying camouflage was to shroud the warehouse in trees by stealthily placing it amid a newly planted poplar forest, simultaneously re-creating the typical suburban condition of a neighborhood that butts up against a plot of undeveloped forested land. Another blending technique wraps the building in an exoskeleton of panelized steel and decorative, faux-gold weapons which, when viewed from the forest path, duplicates the flickering shadows, filtered light, and swaying leaves of the trees. Yet another camouflage tactic disguises the warehouse's service and auxiliary spaces, which sit on the warehouse's roof and serve the storage facilities below, in the style of the suburban neighborhood's homes. As the roof slopes down to ground level and straight into the neighborhood, it appears as if the neighborhood itself, including a street, the houses, yards, and gardens, march up the roof, ending in a cul-de-sac, the quintessential suburban social space. Finally, the reflectivity and repetitive scale of the screen system creates a secure barrier for the collection.

03 03

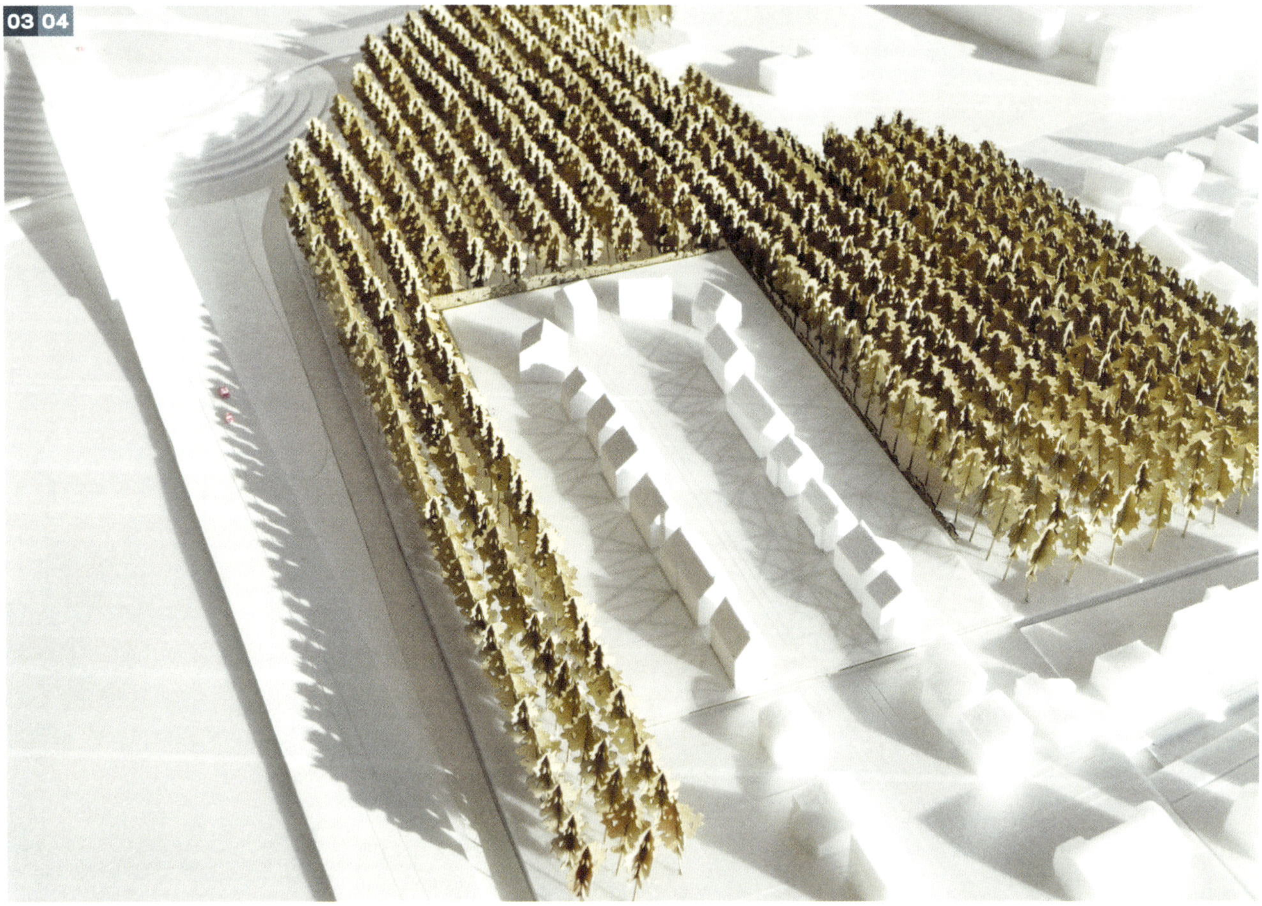

03 04

03 05

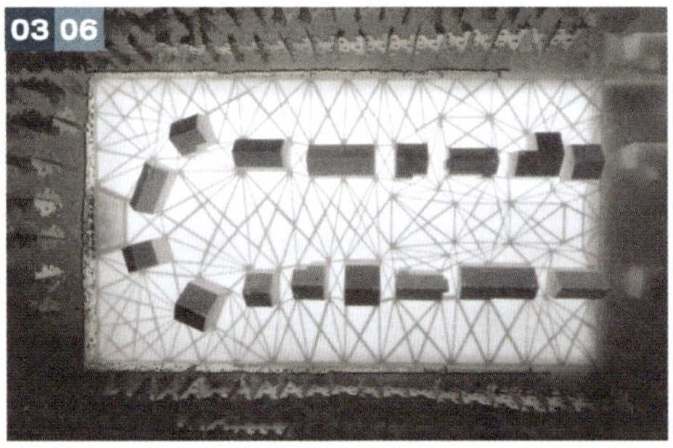

03 06

03|07

03|08

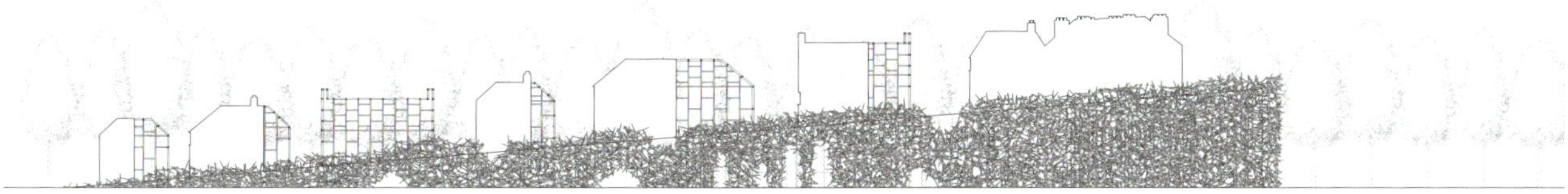

03|09

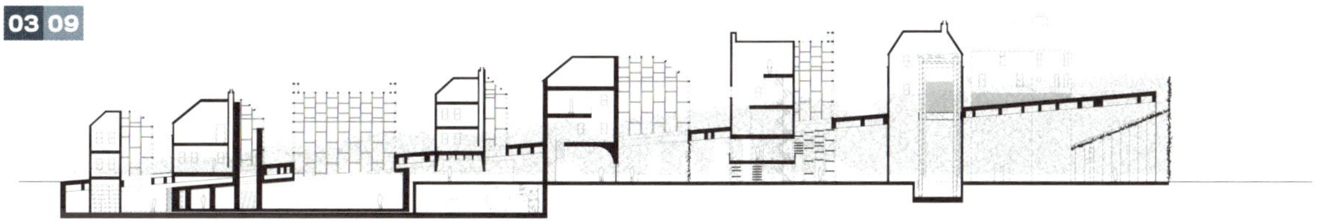

03|10

03.03 An aerial view of the site before (left), next to the site with the storage facility in place (right).

03.04 Aerial model photo.

03.05 View from a car window on the adjacent highway showing the building barely visible through the dense grid of poplar trees.

03.06 Diagrammatic view showing the structural pattern that supports the roof.

03.07 Rendering from the pedestrian approach through the forest. Children from the neighboring suburb play in the woods.

03.08 Elevation showing the building screen, the slope of the building, and the houses on the roof.

03.09 Section showing how the houses function as service space and auxiliary program for the collection below.

03.10 Concept model exploring the use of multiple elements from the collection to create pavilions in the surrounding landscape.

IAN STARLING

THE BRITISH MUSEUM STORAGE TOWER

The world's first national public museum, the British Museum was established in 1753. The initial collection was based on that of Sir Hans Sloane, a physician and naturalist who collected over 71,000 objects, including books, manuscripts, prints, dried flowers, and antiquities from all over the world. Upon his death, he donated his collection to King George II for the benefit of the entire British nation. The museum opened its doors on January 15, 1759, at Montagu House, where it remains to this day.

Over the 250 years of the storied institution's history, the museum's collection has expanded to include over fifteen million historical objects that are not only extremely diverse in their geographical and historical provenance, but also in their form and material, ranging from the Elgin Marbles to a pill to treat the AIDs epidemic. However, due to curatorial considerations and spatial constraints, only 80,000 of the fifteen million artifacts are on display at any given time.

This project for a contemporary, off-site repository for the British Museum in Swindon responds to the dual challenge of creating a publicly accessible storage facility that respects and advances the institution's commitment to preserving both British and global culture for posterity while also addressing the fact that the British Museum as a branded institution has only occupied the museum site in London.

Located adjacent to a suburban shopping center in Swindon, the British Museum Storage Tower is designed to house the collection's undisplayed objects according to their optimal climatic requirements. It has seven distinct climate profiles that correspond to the various objects in the museum. For example, the objects that require cold conditions are located at the bottom of the tower, while the less sensitive objects are farther up. By arranging the objects according to their optimal storage climate, new relationships between the objects give rise to collections that visitors usually would not see.

The tower form optimizes access to the storage spaces by limiting the distance from the stored items to the elevator and also achieves an iconic form in the suburban landscape of Swindon. The iconicity of the tower has not only contemporary relevance but also hearkens back to the landscape paintings of English Romanticism. The British Museum Storage Tower strives to create a contemporary version of artist John Constable's depictions of Salisbury Cathedral in the pristine English landscape.

The British Museum Storage Tower provides a contemporary symbol for the British Museum that advances its institutional mission while retaining its distinctly British character.

04.01 View showing the building from the intersection approaching the Greenbridge Retail Park.

04.02 Diagram illustrating the objects' various material profiles and their corresponding climate zones.

04 01

04 02

current distribution

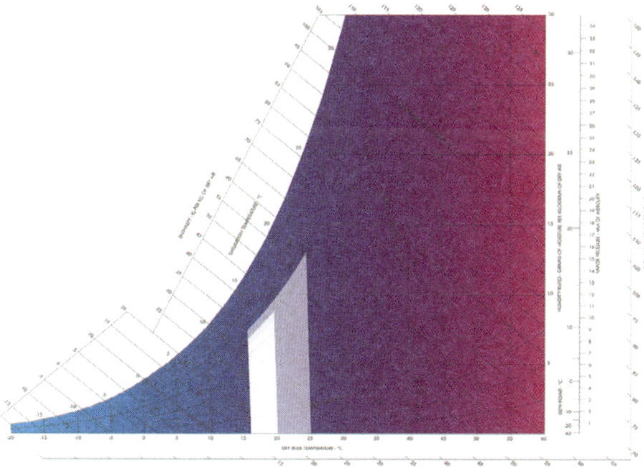

ideal distribution

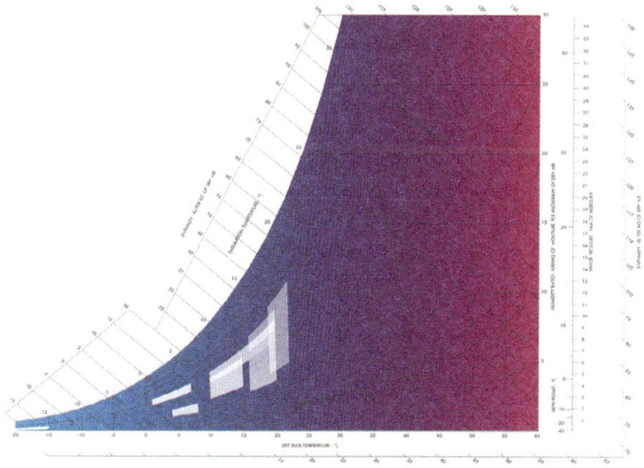

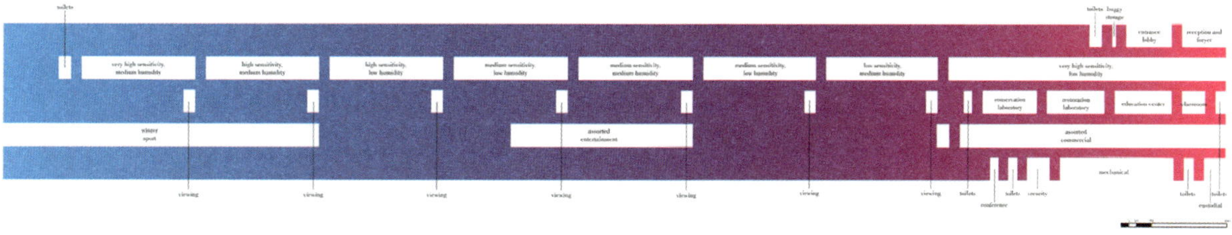

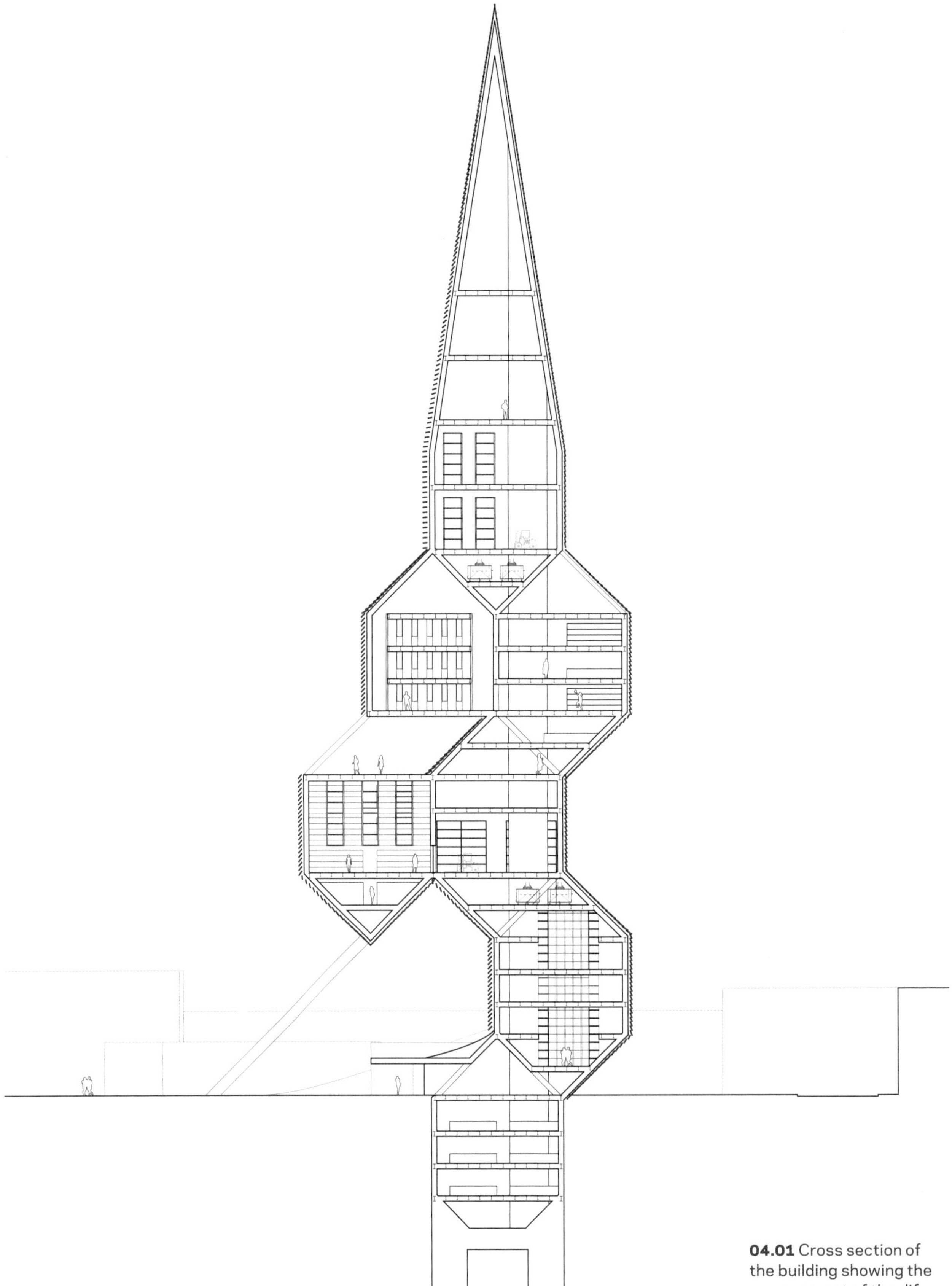

04.01 Cross section of the building showing the arrangement of the different storage areas and climate zones.

04.02 View showing the building's entry.

BINGO

02 INHABITING ARTIFACTS

The artifacts of each collection became a way into, and then a touchstone for, articulating a material culture for each project. Students were encouraged to explore Oldenburg scaling techniques to reconsider the worth of form writ large. Several proposals sample the forms and materials of artifacts, manipulating their scale to create appropriate architectures that reflect the collection. As the Oldenburg scaling was used as a means to validate the facsimiles, the studio asked what benefits come with an ambivalent use of scale? What opportunities are made possible by the specific flexibilities of an inherited form? What role do these exquisite shapes play in regenerating loosely defined, edge-of-town locations?

VINCENT CALABRO

ROYAL ARMOURIES

Locked in an anonymous parking garage in Leeds is one of the largest collections of firearms in the world, the Royal Armouries National Firearms Centre. Since the museum's mission is to archive one of every firearm ever created, the collection is impressive in scale. Currently, the general public can see only a glimpse of this collection. The challenge of this project is to transform a nearly private institution's collection so that it is accessible and visited by the public. Another challenge is the dichotomy of the collection itself, as firearms are both ingenious machines as well as weapons of death and destruction. Furthermore, the center is an active research institution in which forensic testing and firearm research is done.

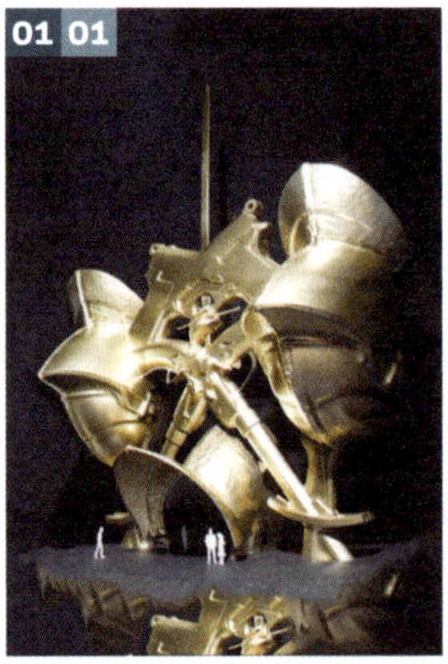

The site is across the street from the former Great Western Railway depot in Swindon. The site has since been converted into an area of commerce and culture containing, among other entities, the Swindon Designer Outlet, the National Trust, the English Heritage, and the Steam Museum of the Great Western Railway. The site for the Royal Armouries National Firearms Centre is a buffer between this retrofitted area and a residential neighborhood.

01.01 Concept model for entrance.

01.02 Rendering of the atrium of the Royal Armouries National Firearms Centre.

The proposed building creates a transition by having two scales. The façade on the residential side of the project is highly fenestrated and thus references the surrounding neighborhoods. The commercial face is a single, swooping gesture that welcomes the public and matches the "re-purposed" Great Western Railway buildings across the street.

Iconic forms from the Royal Armouries carve the roofline, inform the plan, and shape the entryway. The imagery chosen celebrates the history and beauty of the museum's collection. The scale of the elements is varied in a playful manner, allowing people to compare themselves to Beefeaters or pass through a display of the crown jewels. The flat language also magnifies the intensity of the firearms within.

Levels of access and security are key to the project. The collection needs to be accessible to the public but also secure because of the nature of the objects being displayed. A large, central atrium surrounded by firearms permits even the most casual viewer to experience the breadth of the collection. Through key sectional and plan changes, the Royal Armouries in Swindon maintains a balance between public access and active, ongoing research.

01 03

01 04

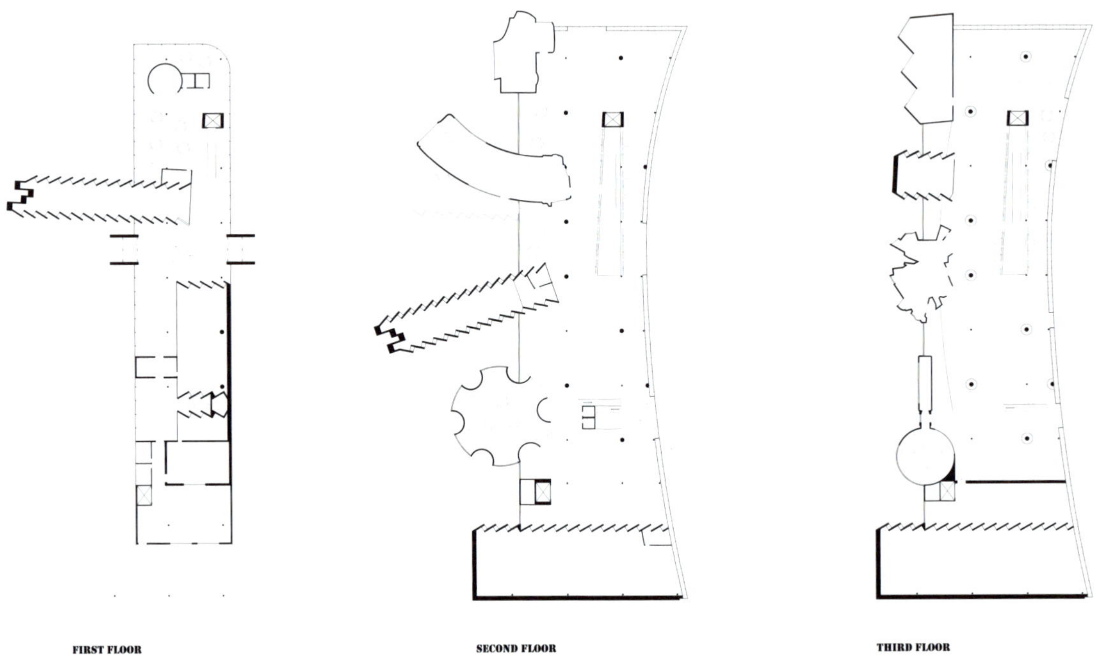

01.03 A conceptual drawing of intentions for the Firearms Centre in Britain.

01.04 Sections of proposed Firearms Centre in Britain.

01.05 Rendering of the west façade.

01 05

01 06

01.06 "Plastic + Fantastic" entrance: This initial entrance design celebrates the history and beauty of the Royal Armouries' collection. The scale of the elements is varied in a playful manner that allows people to compare themselves to Beefeaters or pass through the crown jewels. The flattening of these elements adds to the joyful reading.

02 01

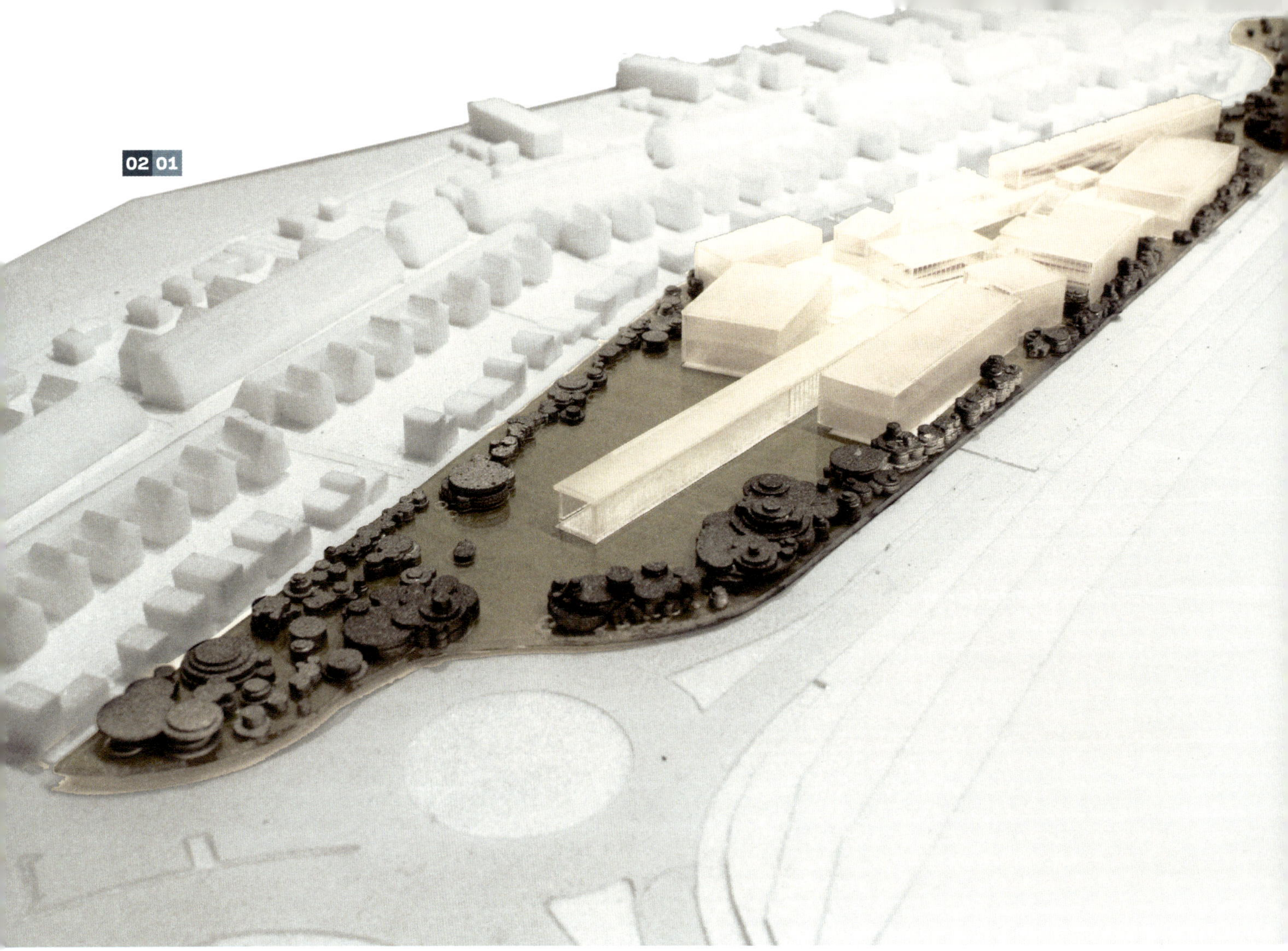

LANE RICK

ROYAL ARMOURIES WALL

Like its original housing in the Tower Wall of London, the Royal Armouries in Swindon is housed behind a protective wall that wraps around the edge of the site. This protective wall invokes the original London home of the Armouries while also distancing the weaponry from the residential neighborhood that backs the site. Within the protective wall, the concrete-and-glass repository pulls away from the metallic wall and breaks down into a cluster of low masses, each containing some portion of the varied collection that makes up the Royal Armouries. For motorists driving on the busy road that runs along the south edge of the site, the wall and masses that rise behind it provide visual interest. For the residents in the row houses to the north of the site, the low profile of the building avoids towering over the houses; further, the wall keeps residents from the constant sight of weaponry, while allowing them to pass through the site.

02 02

The protective steel-clad wall that runs along the outer edge of the site bears a physical resemblance to both tower turrets and oversized gun barrels. Though the wall acts as a visual screen to the surrounding neighborhood, it is permeable, and residents can cut through the site, as many do. Cuts and disintegrations in the wall correspond to those paths that are already used as throughways. Behind the wall is an open green space. In addition to enclosing this landscape, the wall provides seating. It disintegrates into a field of sculptural masses and houses a few public programmatic elements, including a restaurant, café, and an information center.

02.01 Final model of the Royal Armouries repository.

02.02 A Beefeater and a gun, juxtaposed.

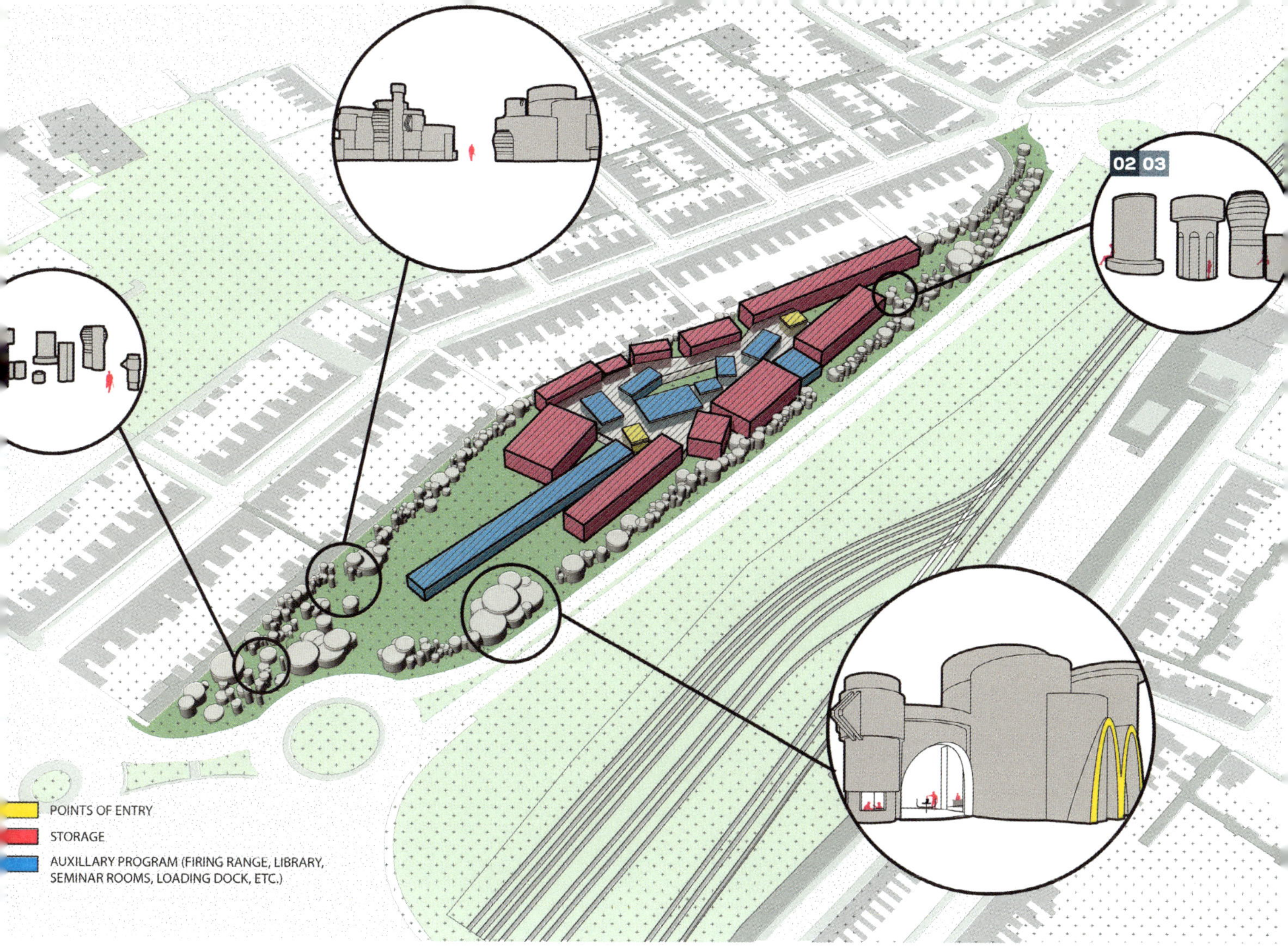

02.03 Drawing denoting the different functions that occur within the building.

02.04 Entrance model of the barreled wall.

02.05 Drawing investigating possible juxtapositions between the objects in storage and the building itself.

The building itself is broken into many smaller masses. Rather than being confronted at all times with the expansive collection, the visitor is able to narrow his or her focus to the specific objects in one or two rooms at a time. The concrete storage rooms are connected by a secure corridor. Where the storage intersects with the corridor, glass windows allow visitors to see inside the storage areas to view more of the vast collection before moving to a smaller room. The constant interplay between the collection and the specific, human-scaled objects is reinforced by the layout of the building: the storage rooms are clustered at the center of the site and skewed to different angles, which contributes to a livelier corridor by permitting visitors to see into many rooms at once.

The two secure points of entry into the facility are both pushed back into the heart of the building; visitors slide between the storage masses to the entrances. From the entry chamber, the visitor is granted clearance to move through the adjacent corridor to view the collection and access a portion of the collection in a specific room. In addition to the storage space, an exhibition space, a library, and a couple of study rooms sit within the structure and back an intimate interior courtyard. Accessible to all visitors of the building, these parts of the program are pulled away from the storage toward the inner courtyard. Public functions occur in these areas, including seminars, tours, a shooting range, and a small library, as well as offices and restoration labs.

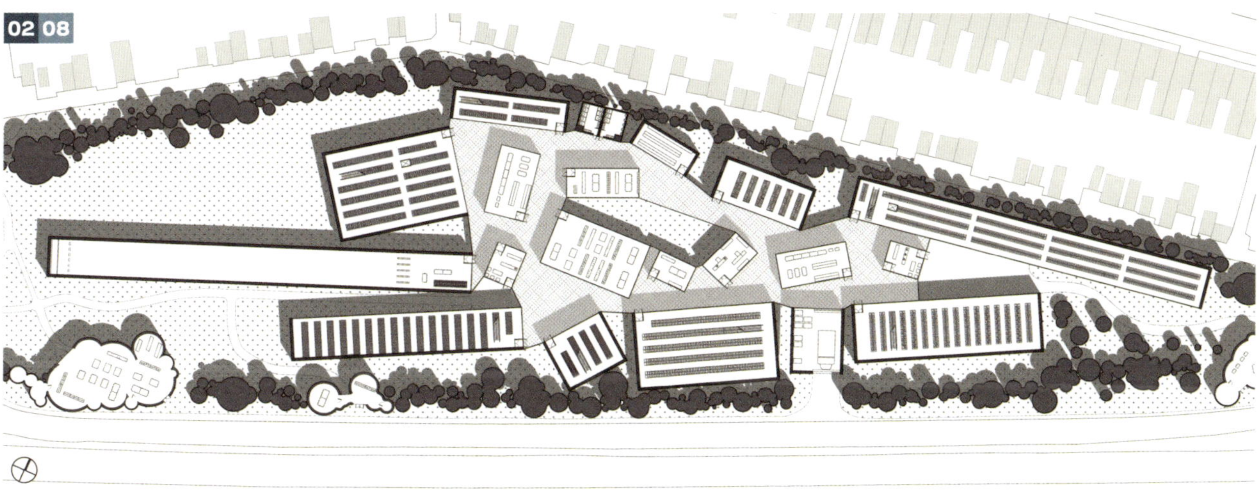

02.06 View of the barreled wall and building from the road.

02.07 View of the entrance from inside the barreled wall.

02.08 Ground floor plan of the repository.

FRANCESCO GALETTO

THE BRITISH MUSEUM STORAGE SHRINES

This project proposes a storage facility for the British Museum by connecting different ethnic, cultural, and religious groups with the eight million artifacts from its collection. These objects compose the largest collection of historical artifacts. Though the motto of the museum is "Of the world, for the world," less than one percent of the objects are shown to the public at any given time.

The British Museum is notorious for possessing artifacts of arguable ownership that were collected by imperialists during times of conflict, such as the Elgin Marbles, claimed by Greece, and the Benin Bronzes, claimed by Nigeria. While the collection holds many disputed objects, none are more notorious than the eight artifacts defined by the museum as "secret/sacred" items — in fact, they are so protected that only high officials, typically clergy of a specific sect, are allowed to handle the objects.

One such set of secret/sacred artifacts are the Ethiopian Talbots, claimed by the Ethiopian Orthodox Church. These talbots are said to have been stored in the ark of the covenant with the Ten Commandments. In Ethiopia, the talbots were used in religious parades by the high clergy, who carried them wrapped in purple velvet on their heads. The talbots, now located in the British Museum collection, cannot be venerated by the church and its followers as they were intended to be.

The project proposes a new storage facility that facilitates the veneration of the eight secret/sacred artifacts. The proposed facility hopes to bring together religious and secular pilgrims from around the world in an attempt to increase the veneration of all the objects, with a particular focus on the eight secret/sacred objects.

The artifacts are placed in shrines encircling the general collection. The shrines are each relevant to the architecture, culture, and ceremony of each object and are accessed from the exterior of the building through a field of sculpted columns, creating nine distinct entrances to the facility. Each shrine's façade is embossed in concrete, becoming both a billboard and monument for the storage facility.

The storage facility is surrounded by a field of topiary and sculpted columns which express the evolution of civilization through different themes, such as money, communication, and weapons. Each themed column is constructed from objects represented within the museum. For example, the money column is constructed from shells, coins, and credit cards, all objects that illustrate civilizations' evolving relationship with money. The topiary and columns demarcate a recreational zone and rural landscape for the surrounding community.

03.01 Concept collage of a pilgrimage site for the archive facility.

03.02 View of the entrance to the facility.

03.03 A collage showing the initial view a pilgrim or visitor has of the archive. One of the sacred rooms is accessible behind the façade.

03.04 Bird's-eye and worm's-eye axonometric drawings of the archive.

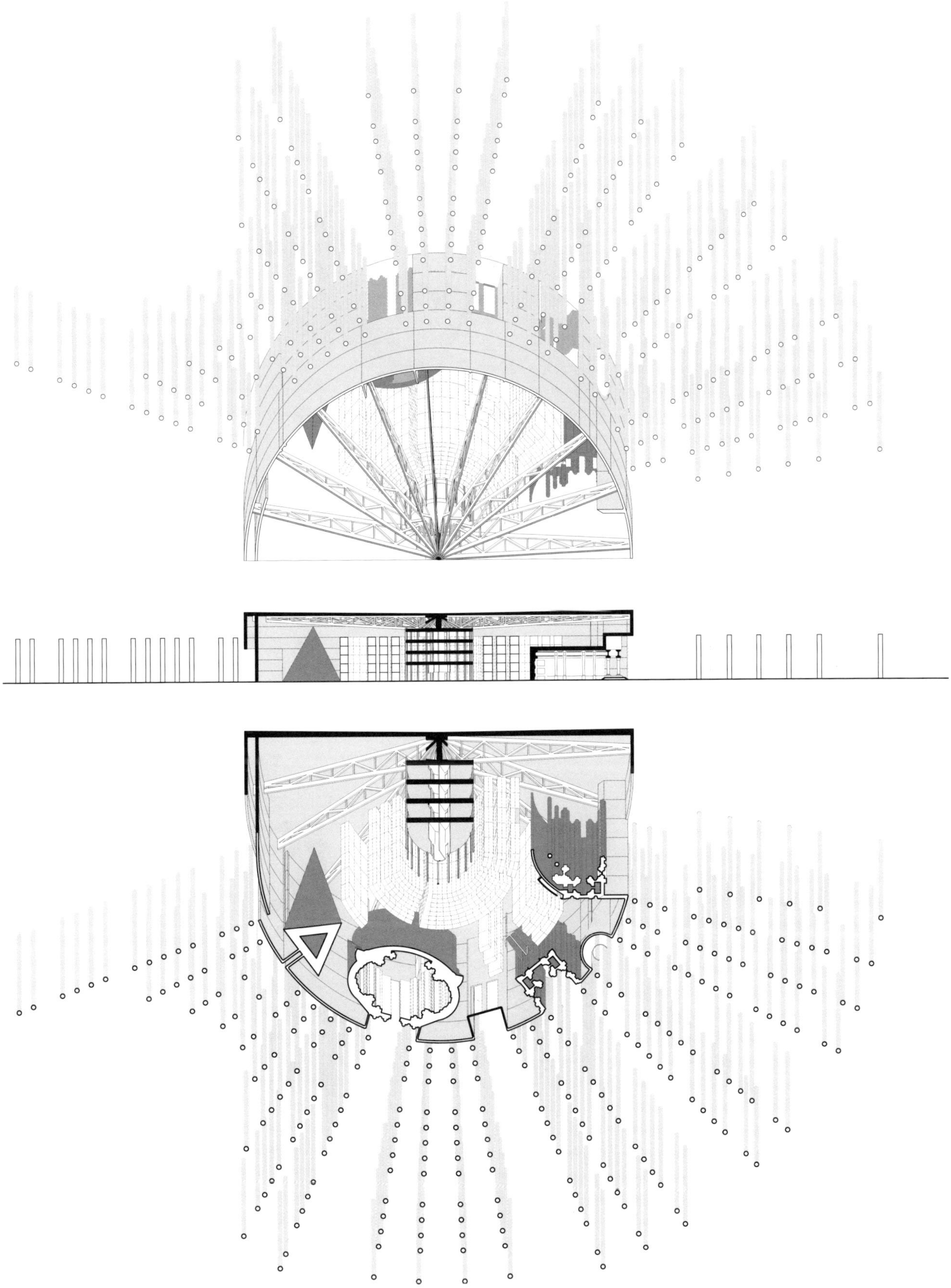

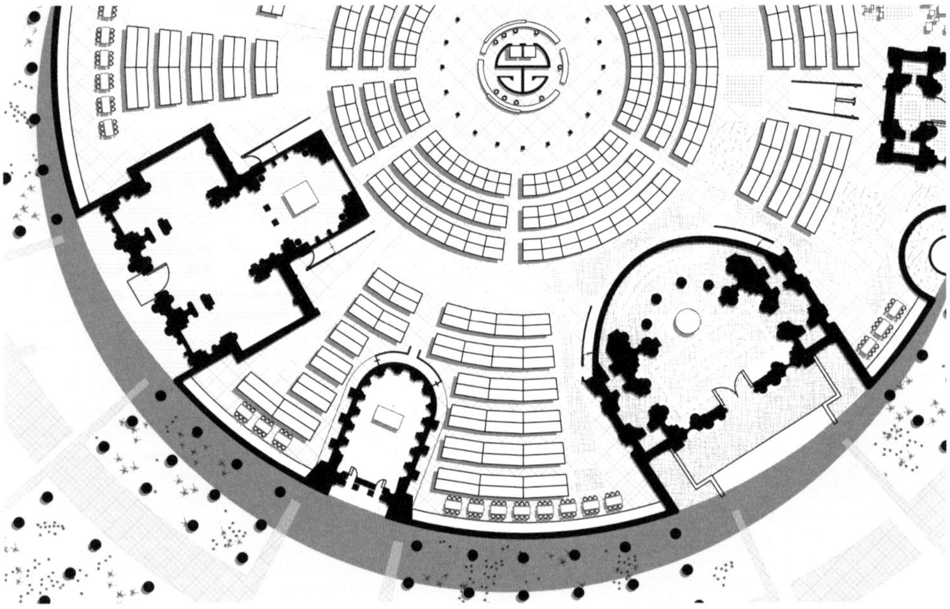

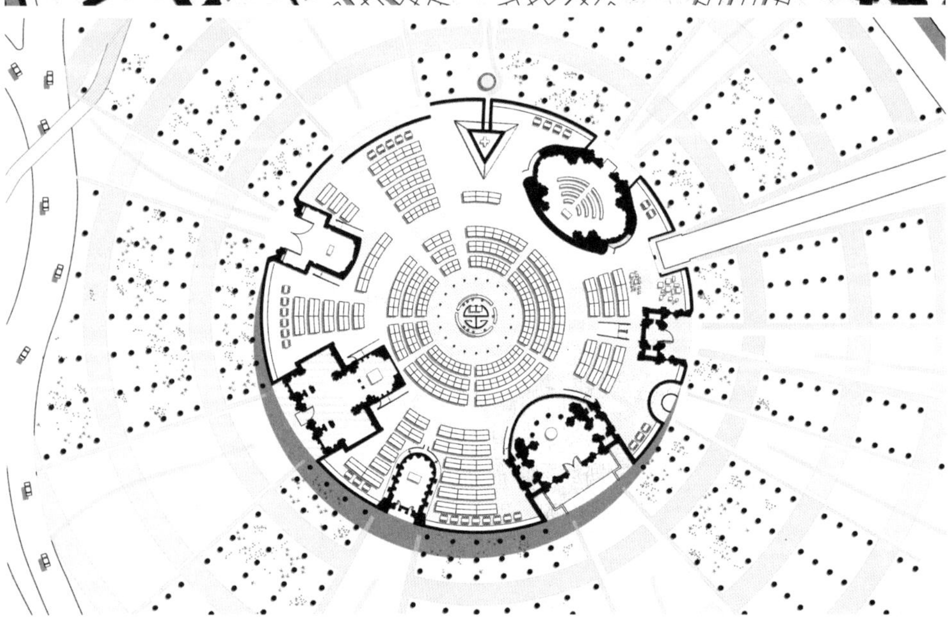

03|05

03.05 Detailed plans showing how the flooring changes with the different objects within the museum.

03.06 Initial entrance to the new archive facility.

03.07 Interior perspective of the archive. The storage racks are reflected in the administrative core located at the center of the building.

03.08 Preliminary conceptual drawing stating the goals of the project.

a good multi faith-multi cultural facility needs...

1. a green space for people of a growing swindon
2. a place to grub at in the park
3. a great hall for with multiple entrances for different users
4. a storage facility for the espanding British Museum
5. a high and low education facility
6. visibility between the underground and the outside
7. a gallery-a wall of wonder objects from around the world
8. private and secret/sacred storage- makes facility a pilgrimage site
9. a pure room for ceremonies by pilgrims using objects
10. a place for rest for the pilgrims
11. a kitchen to cook and share food of the world
12. provides job for swindon
13. great hall also doubles as performance space
14. natural light to illuminate hall during the day
15. park to bridge motor way
16. pure room to be atmospheric and allow the outdoors in

03 ACCOMMODATING PROCESSES

With unparalleled access to the inner workings of institutions in the U.K., the studio was able to understand the limits set by the confines of existing archive buildings and their supporting infrastructure. Through research and dialogue with archivists and curators, the student projects became charged with an understanding of their chosen institution's identity and the elements that make each one tick. Often with reference to Cedric Price, proposals forged new processes of cultural production based around some of the nation's most valued assets and suggested new models of organization. At the heart of the work was an investigation into the ways in which physical and virtual control structures are enmeshed in popular culture.

ERIK HERRMANN

BRITISH LIBRARY CATALOGUING CENTRE

The death of the book was a premature declaration, and the challenges facing the British Library are proof. Since its inception in the early eighteenth century, the library has been responsible for storing a copy of every book printed in the British Empire. As the collection continues to grow, the rate of cataloging has been dramatically outpaced by the backlog of books arriving daily at the library's main branch, at St. Pancras.

The New British Library Cataloguing Centre proposes a radical, social, and interaction-based model for the intake, cataloging, and storage of books. The facility is strategically located in the town of Swindon, an hour's train ride from London. With cheaper land costs and an undeveloped site with rail access, Swindon can provide the British Library with a satellite cataloging center capable of handling the tremendous amount of printed material and ephemera produced by new modes of self-publishing. The proposed Cataloguing Centre is organized as a large, open warehouse on the public level, with direct access to the latest acquisitions available to patrons. At the heart of the complex is a sorting pit, where new arrivals are tagged. The warehouse is filled with a series of towers that contain study spaces at the lower levels and fixed storage at the upper levels.

01.01 View from interior of the Cataloguing Centre, looking across the sorting pit and towers beyond.

01.02 Diagrammatic analysis of Wikipedia that compares the formal start page and the open-source content pages.

01 02

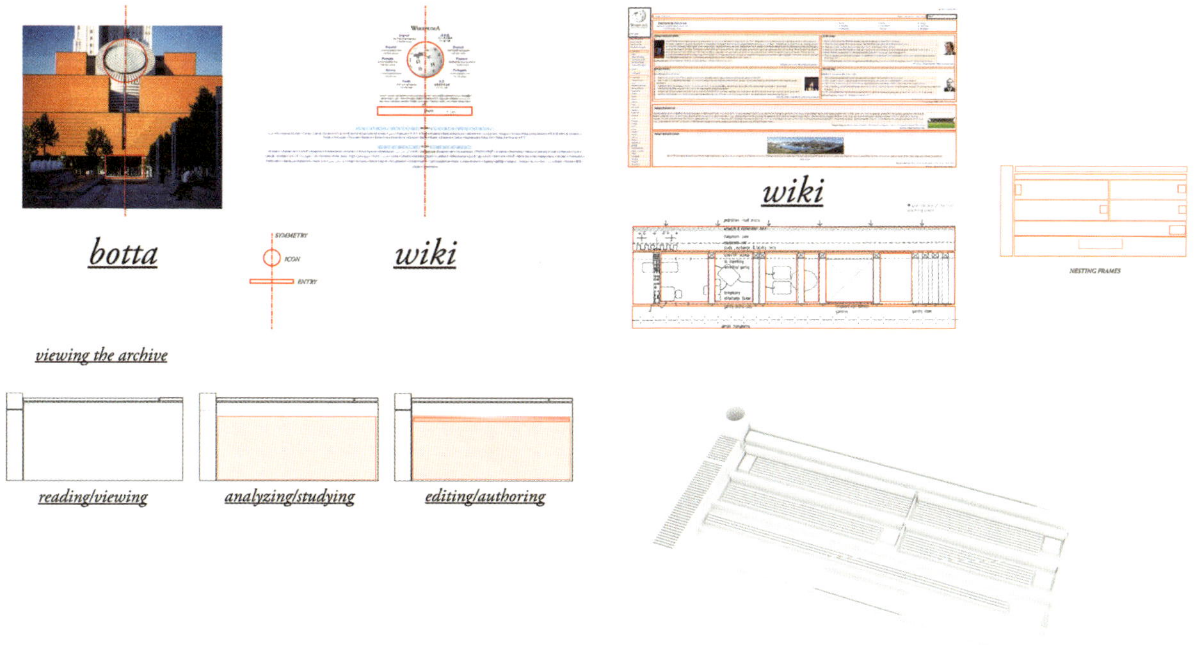

3d wikipedia

01 03

01 04

01 05

01.03 Final montage elevation of the Cataloguing Centre, inspired by vintage British Railway posters.

01.04 Elevation of initial entry study model sampling elements from the British Library's collection and building at St. Pancras as well as IKEA store.

01.05 Final night view of the Cataloguing Centre from the rail yard.

01.06 Sections of the British Library at Swindon.

01.07 Plans of the British Library at Swindon.

01 06

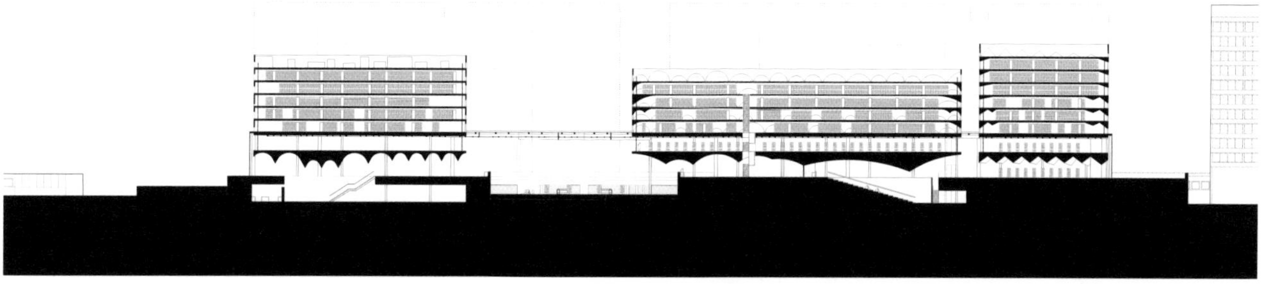

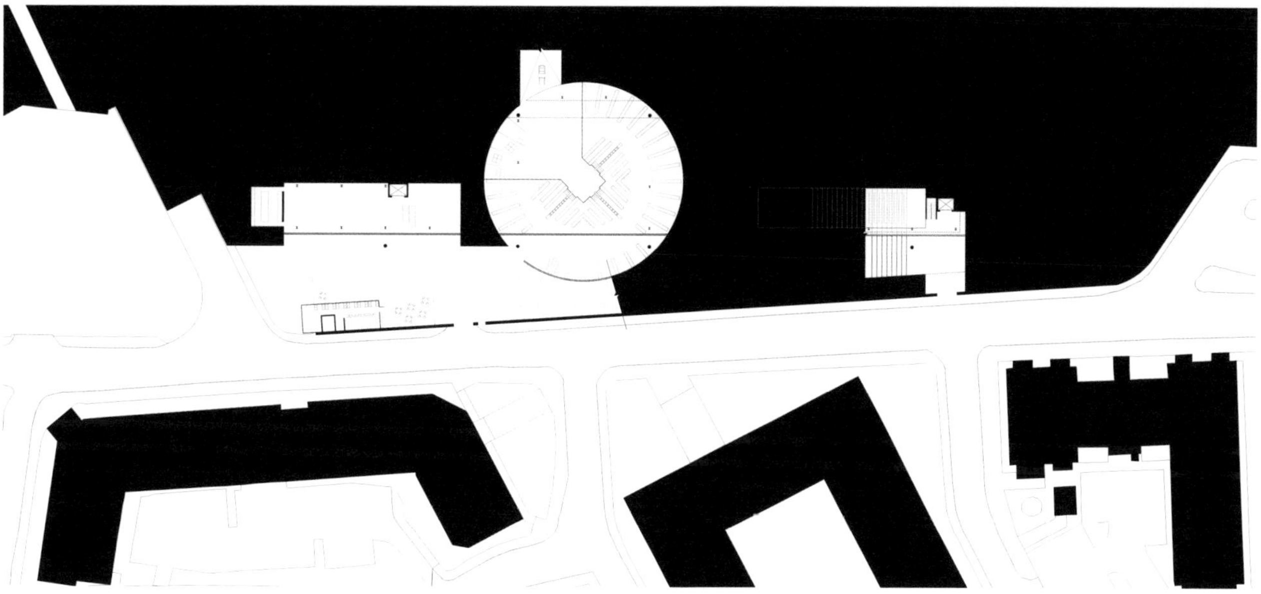

01 07

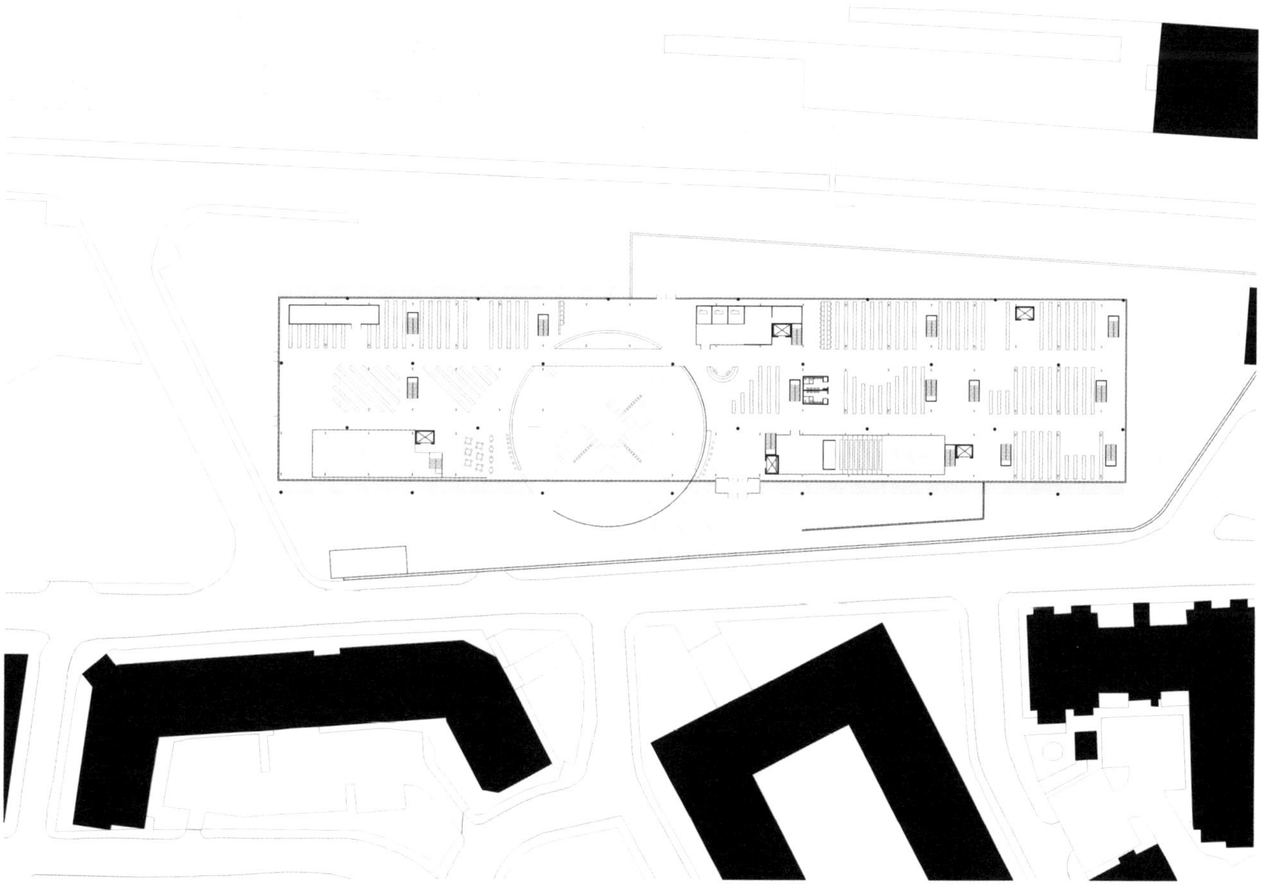

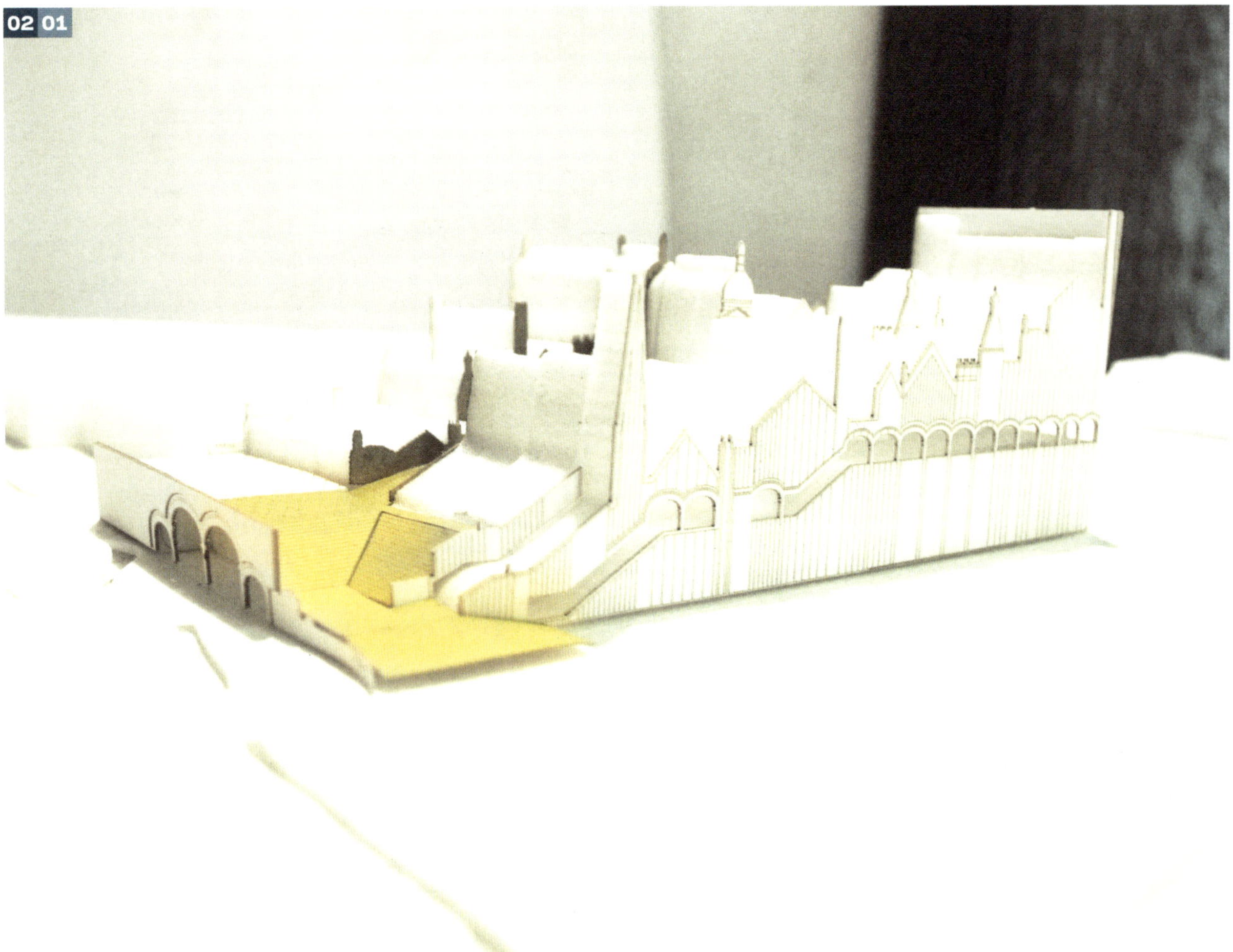

DANIELLE DURYEA

TATE MERCHANDISE

This project proposes a Tate Merchandise production and storage center for the Tate Gallery in the Greenbridge Retail Park of Swindon. More than most museum institutions, the Tate has spent a considerable investment on its branding and advertising strategies. This project offers a critique of the commercialization of art and the "museumification" of gift shops.

The Tate Gallery receives the least amount of its funding (38 percent) from the British government grant-in-aid program compared to the percentage of grant-in-aid funds received by other, major London-based institutions, such as the Royal Armouries (82.5 percent), the Victoria and Albert (60 percent), the National Gallery (78 percent), the British Museum (56.5 percent), and the National Portrait Gallery (43 percent). The shortcomings of government aid have resulted in a restructuring of the Tate toward a commodity-driven business model. Tate Enterprises is a subsidiary of the Tate Gallery and oversees the publishing, shops, and catering divisions. While Tate Enterprises doesn't generate the majority of the revenue for the Tate Gallery, the products generated develop brand recognition and repeat visits. Tate Merchandise operates as an integral part of Tate Enterprises as it houses the production and storage of objects for the gift shop. Additionally, the program of Tate Merchandise integrates a public component of shopping to allow the consumption of Tate products to occur simultaneously

02.01 Final 1:200 scale model.

02.02 View of the gift shop looking into the production space.

02.03 An early program adjacency diagram of shopping and production in the "fun palace."

02 02

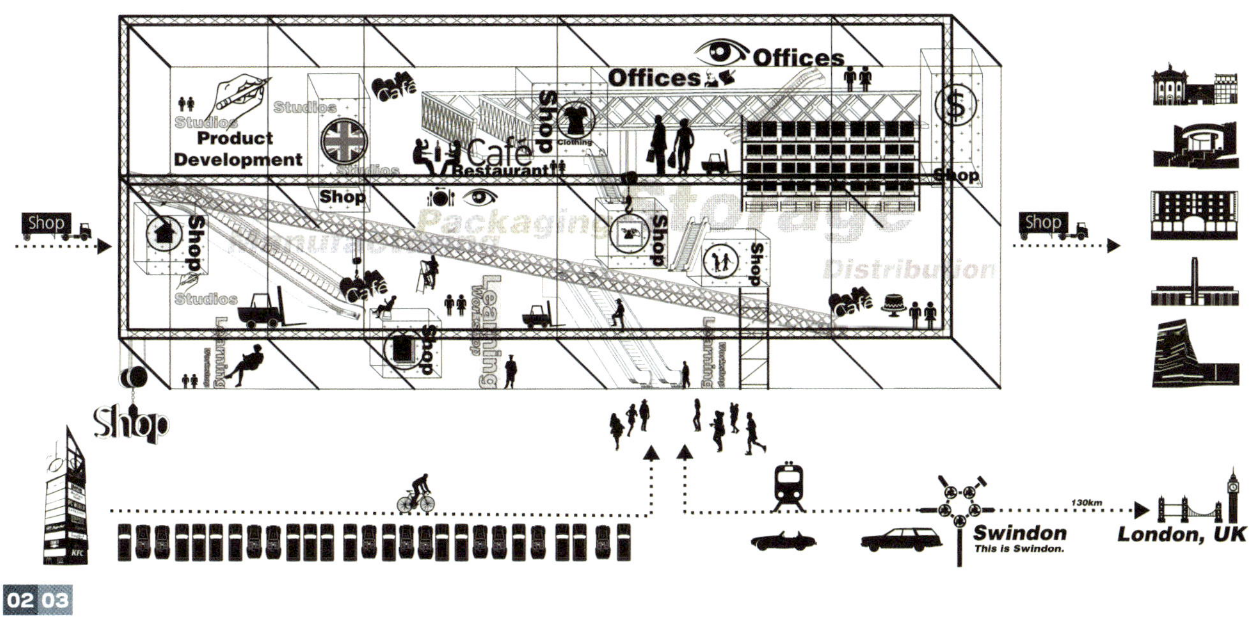
Offices
Offices
Studios
Studios
Product Development
Café
Café
Restaurant
Clothing
Shop
Shop
Packaging
Storage
Distribution
Studios
Learning
Learning
Shop
Swindon
This is Swindon.
130km
London, UK

02 03

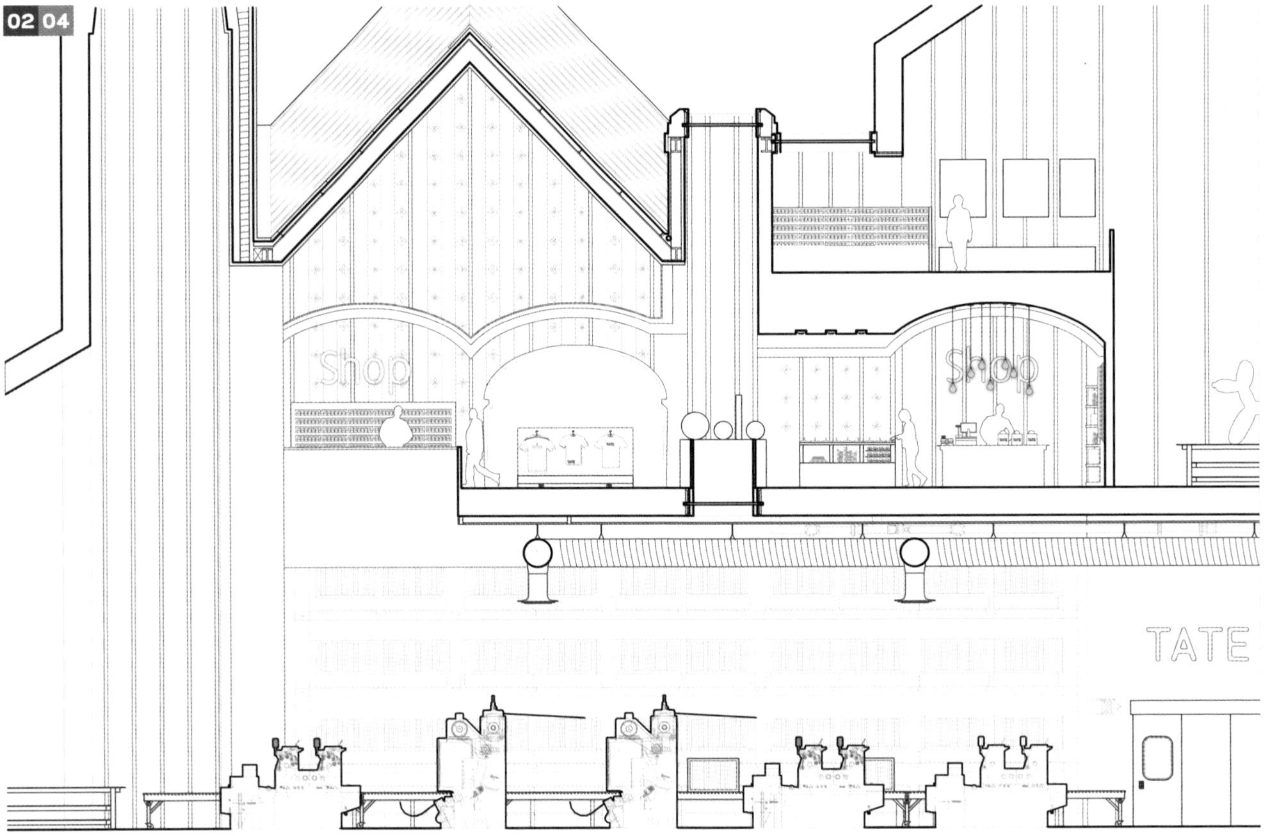

with production. The items produced at Tate Swindon range from large-scale, mass-printed reproductions to custom replications commissioned by artists. The diverse range, from high culture to mass pop-culture art, is reflected in the reproductions at every scale.

The formal strategy for Tate Merchandise samples and combines the four Tate galleries as an extrusion atop a generic big box. The ambition to sample the existing forms was driven by the Tate's strategy of repeated logo and brand recognition. Instead of repeating the Tate logo, Tate Swindon repeats and rearranges the building forms to become a town of consumption over production. An extrusion in one direction addresses the urban main street with a flat, "billboard" façade, while the more articulated façade designates the public entry. Cars enter the retail park and approach the Tate Merchandise from the corner, allowing both façades to be read in contrast to one another. Co-opting the imagery of the Tate galleries into a single façade reduces the glorified image of the museum to a decorated storage shed.

02.04 Section through shop and the production space.

02.05 Early process model of the grand entrance to the Tate Merchandise.

02.06 Diagram showing the Tate's funding.

02.07 Tate funding diagram: public portion.

02.08 Tate funding diagram: private portion.

02.09 Concept diagram shows the "town" of shopping above the big-box warehouse.

02.10 The Tate's history in the form of a timeline.

02.11 Tate imagery: examples of items from the Tate collection and buildings recontextualized as gift-shop commodities.

02 05

02 06

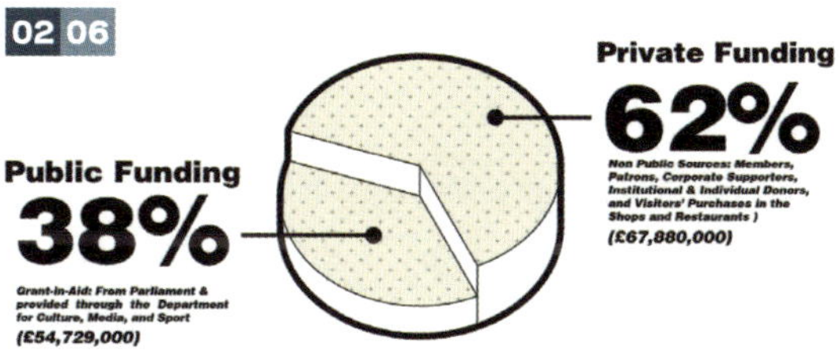

02 07

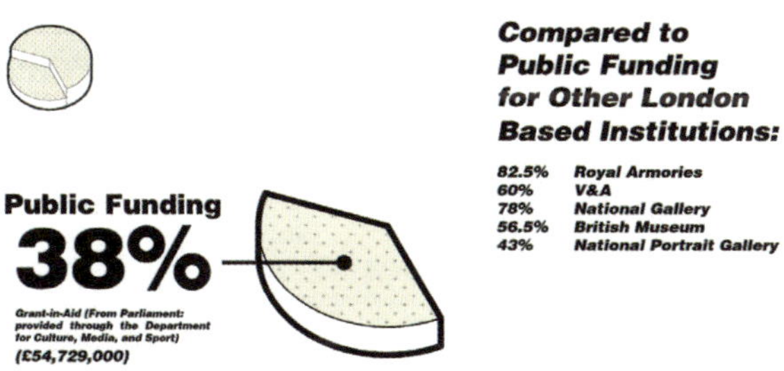

02 08

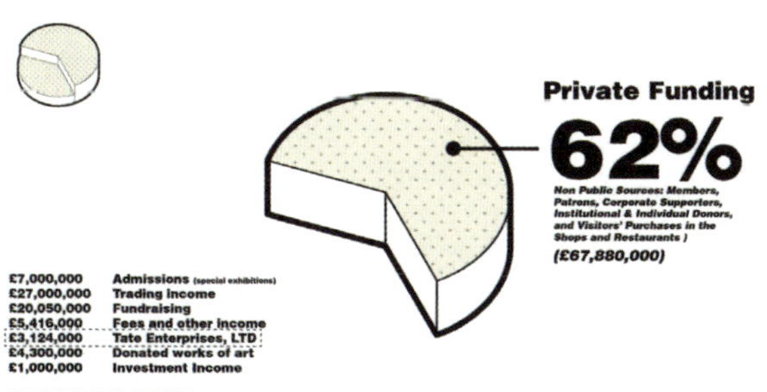

02 09

02 10

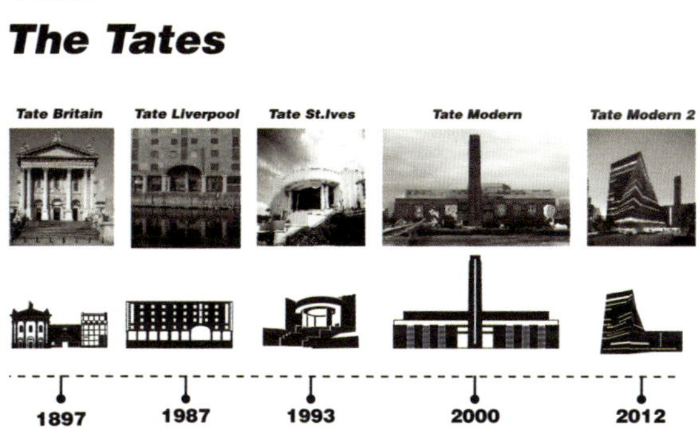

02 11

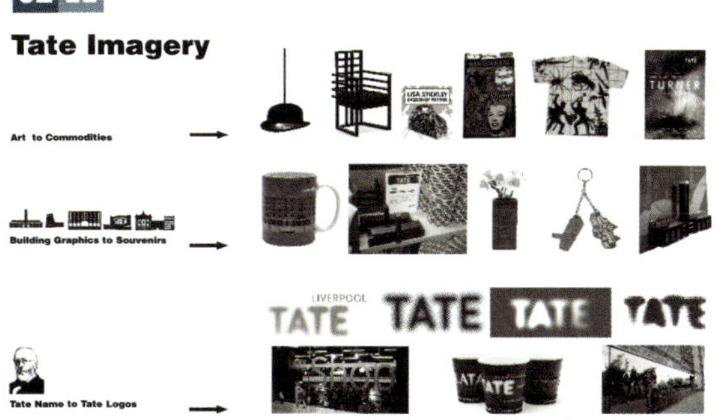

studio work

115

accommodating processes

Hernán Díaz
Alonso

Type versus Species

Xefirotarch/Hernán Díaz Alonso, Still Flesh.

Hernán Díaz Alonso the founder of the Los Angeles-based firm of Xefirotarch was the Louis I. Kahn Visiting Assistant Professor at Yale teaching and advanced studio in Fall 2010. He was interviewed by architectural critic, Nina Rappaport about aesthetics and his projects.

Nina Rappaport: In a subtle way, your teaching and work is about a new or renewed aesthetic that is difficult. It is not a totally pleasing image or composition, nor is it easily comprehended; rather, it is a more intellectual concept for an aesthetic theory. How do you define this aesthetic theory, and how do you teach so that it becomes part of the vocabulary in design and architecture? Hernán Díaz Alonso: I've been teaching for ten years in the States, at three schools. In a weird way, I think it's like a wild animal. I never feel like I'm fully in control, in the sense that I still don't consider myself a teacher; I see myself as the director of a laboratory. My methodology changes over time, but there are recurring logics.

But you need some kind of method and direction, even if it morphs into something else over time? Yes, you do need it. Whatever I teach is based on where I want to go, not what I know. Teaching is always like an adventure—to quote the Joker from The Dark Knight: "Do I look like I have a plan?" The idea behind one project becomes the genesis for the next, toward a different direction. The problem of aesthetics has been a natural progression in my thinking. Since graduating with my bachelor's degree in Argentina, I've been obsessed with form. I was first attracted to the autonomy of form as a main discourse in architecture, but, over time, I have realized that I have to refine it and become more specific.

Your work is also very cinematic, as if it were meant more for the screen than for the real

world. When did you switch your interest from filmmaking to architecture? When I was eighteen, I wanted to become a filmmaker. But the school in Argentina was not going well, so I took classes in architecture to get credit and then went back to film school. A teaching assistant showed me the catalog of the *Deconstructivist* show at MoMA, where I first saw the work of Coop Himmelb(l)au, Zaha Hadid, and Enric Miralles, and that work influenced my decision to continue studying architecture. Then, when I started using computers and animation, it was an interesting opportunity to start exploring earlier interests. The problem became less about geometry controlling form and more about the idea of image as the vehicle for the production of form. That is what the software is for: it produces images so simulation overtakes representation.

Back to the question of aesthetics: What is your interpretation of beauty, and do you think there should be a general definition or comprehension of beauty? If you're interested in the problem of form, one way or another you're interested in beauty in the most classical definition of it. Evolving from that idea, I realized I was really interested in the beautiful, rather than beauty. Of course the theories are similar, but beauty has a specific philosophical and intellectual implication. To me, the beautiful is a present moment; maybe something is beautiful, and then it can stop being beautiful. The work I was producing along those lines was not considered beautiful by most people.

Why is that? I think the work operates with a different logic, with certain autonomous entities that have to do with a methodology that produces a particular kind of aesthetic. So the word *grotesque* comes into play.

If you want to produce something that is beautiful and you have an aesthetic that defines what is beautiful, can you then control the creation of that aesthetic? Yes, absolutely.

For example, some people think the silver skeleton ring you wear is beautiful, and others think it's hideous. That is the difference between beauty and the beautiful. We all agree on beauty: there are rules defining my ring as beautiful maybe for some, but not for others. But we are producing beautiful work; if not, I would not be interested. I have never been interested in an intelligent or a strategic architecture. I have a very primitive approach. For me, it's about a sense of arousal or lust. I need to feel excited about the things I produce, and I want other people to feel excited. How you do that is a different thing. The work that became "grotesque" gave people a reaction. And of course, if we want to go deep and be specific, which I never like to do much, this has to do with affect. The grotesque is an interesting notion because we tend to confuse grotesque with something ugly or disgusting, which is not the case. The meaning of the word relates to Goya's paintings of the black period because they didn't fit within the aesthetic canon of the time. I like the duality between those two meanings. Grotesque is an emerging quality. I don't think you can produce grotesque; I think something becomes grotesque. The sense or notion of a horrific quality, the production of horror and fear, is interesting because there's an excitement. The horrific is something you can choreograph in one project. The options of what we find beautiful, exciting, or arousing are more complex than they used to be. I think beauty and anger, beauty and perversion, can co-exist.

What is your perspective on biomimcry in architecture and design? Some of your early work looked like interior body parts; Was that conscious? I'm interested in organs and cancers, and I'm interested in plastic surgery. I never considered my work in relation to biology because I never look at those things directly. I always look through cinematic versions of everything, so that's why I always say my work is more cinematic than biological. Let's say my work looks like blood and coagulation. But I would not look at the real thing; I would look at vampire movies and figure out the cinematic effect of blood coagulation. So, if I want to look into plants, I would look at them on the Discovery Channel. As Jeff Kipnis said, "If you want to learn how to paint an apple, you don't study apples. You study other people's paintings of apples." I'm interested in the transformation of the things I'm interested in through image editing, so my work is cinematic.

Do you sometimes design this way for a shock effect? It's certainly not in the forefront of my thinking. I've always been a big fan of the fashion designer Alexander McQueen. He killed himself at my age, during a midlife crisis. I think his work at the beginning was all about shock — and probably my early work was, too — but then he began to refine

Xefirotarch/Hernán Díaz Alonso, Teatro Colón, Bogotá, Colombia

Xefirotarch/Hernán Díaz Alonso, Teatro Colón, Bogotá, Colombia.

it and became incredibly sophisticated, rather than shocking. I think it became deep work that elicited an emotional reaction. I would like to think of my work that way, too.

What do you mean exactly by sophistication, and how does it relate to the beautiful? I'm actually more obsessed with the problem of sophistication and virtuosity than the problem of beauty. If the work has a high level of sophistication — even if the origin is something disgusting, perverse, cancerous, or rotten — if you filter it to a high level of sophistication and precision, then it becomes something incredibly sublime and acquires a whole different dimension. There's almost a sublime quality that comes into it.

Why are you interested in the sublime, and how do you define it? I have a much more visceral reaction to the world than a manifesto; I just grab sublime as a sound bite. We do not add to the sublime era and then figure out what that means. The way I look at things is much more myopic. I'm obsessed with "misfit" as a methodology and working with incredibly precise moments of formal geometry within completely imprecise, drastic conditions.

How do you apply this to an architectural or industrial design project? We are working on two families of things now. One is a chair with completely independent structure and skin. We are using a three-dimensional ornament: roses that get chemically treated and then frozen. The flowers decay almost to the edge of rotten, and then we freeze them, so the surface is maintained. The work is taking on an idea of the romantic as the natural progression of things. We are also designing a silverware collection. Next year, we will design a small architecture space for the Centre Pompidou, which is a combination between the two projects. The silverware collection is incredibly precise and almost baroque in its saturation of formal maneuvers, and the chair is both very rustic and aggressive. It has conditions on the surface that I've never addressed, supported by an incredibly precise structure. I'm interested in those kinds of "misfits" as well as the problem of multiple techniques and aesthetics in conflict and friction. It has to do with the idea of the beautiful and the horrific, a lust that has a stunning quality.

Do you want to get back into cinema now? Yes. Actually, I think the work can do all of that. I consider myself a designer more than an architect. I like to design stuff. Sometimes it happens to be a building or

or a pavilion for PS1, sometimes it's product design, sometimes it's a book, sometimes it's cartoons for kids — right now, we're developing that. The main reason I stayed in architecture was Zaha Hadid. She was incredibly important as one of the first architects to really make a big deal about the image, the painting. But I live absolutely in the present. I have no interest in historic validation, although it is worth knowing the precedents and architectural history.

Are your commissions, such as the museum pavilion for TBA21, moving you toward becoming a building architect? Francesca Von Hasburg, who commissioned my firm to make one of three pavilions for different artists and architects, let us make ours in the shape of a small building, rather than a pavilion. It is the size of a big house, with a small apartment for an artist-in-residence. I have a tendency to work completely in the present. One reason we don't get many projects is, every time one starts to take shape, I lose interest and want to rework it. The pavilion was based on principles of cell mutation and aggregation as an interaction between variations of a single thing. But now I'm much more interested in the logic of "misfit," or not such coherent elements, so we are contaminating the pavilion with this new idea of the misfit. Projects are not isolated conditions; they are part of a family of things we are working on.

What new projects have been places of further exploration in a trajectory of your work? One new project is an interior for Boeing in Seattle in collaboration with Alex McDowell, a production designer, he did the film, *Minority Report*. The project belongs to previous issues of image and cinematic quality. Other projects include series of chairs, couches, tables, and lamps, which are more in sync as art works. We have some commissions for art as well, one for the Ritz Carlton in Miami, and a competition for a new library in Finland. This building has different species that are put together in a monstrous way, like Frankenstein. Then there is one made out of meat.

Why is it that meat is been an obsession of yours lately? Meat is cut into organized form so the work has lo-fi/hi-fi in terms of form and a high level of aesthetic and beauty; but it comes out of an aggressive and borderline torturous methodology. There are some cases, as in the ritual of the bullfight, where there is a primary brutal act and it is also a sophisticated method. It has to do with a latent desire to reclaim humanism and corruption with a close fit with the computer. Philosophically, if you think about the Renaissance idea to create perfection out of imperfect techniques, we are the opposite, we develop technologies from the computer that have a latent desire to produce imperfection and mechanisms to reclaim a humanist sense.

Xefirotarch/Hernán Díaz Alonso, Helsinki Library, Helsinki, Finland, 2012.

How has the acceptance and the interest in your work changed? The culture has changed around the understanding of our work as more clients accept it. I don't think anything is that shocking anymore, so it is not about producing something ugly. It is more about the means and the refinement of the work.

Why do you like teaching? In the end, you have to work as a teacher with what interests you. In that sense, the students are working on what you're working on. But they're taking life on, as well. I'm always interested in having the students feel committed to the absolutely pure state of being an architect. But to achieve that, they really need to be willful and to play and to have fun. There has to be an ambition to produce an alternative quality that has to do more with contemporary culture than anything else. The rules of what we consider erotic or sensual have nothing to do with what they were a century ago; we are kind of like monsters in constant mutation. What fascinates me about computers is that, if you look historically at any aesthetic exercise — and this is what I'm interested in working on with the students — they are about making a fake sense of perfection based on imperfect techniques, in painting, sculpting, architecture, Palladio, whatever. Today, we have these absolutely perfect machines with one hundred percent precision, and I'm obsessed with producing an imprecise aesthetic with them, like a reverse logic.

How have the restrictions and the need for a client in architecture informed your work? Even when I do product design or animation, my logic is that of an architect.

As much as I play at trying to break away from the boundaries and restrictions, they are there. The funny thing is, I always like the students to think of that, too. I am incapable of thinking about an abstract problem without a client or a competition or a site or a square-footage program. However insane or radical the work might look to other people, it always comes out of trying to figure out the problem. That is why I like architecture and could not be an artist. The problem will be the concept of "misfit" and collapsing structures. I'm going to be thinking about those implications. I can only do what I do.

Type Versus Species, or the Relevance of Architectural Mutation

Historically, architecture begins with a concept and an overall typological strategy in which each type possesses a preconception of its own deterministic history. As an alternative, this studio examines the possibility of generating architectural form as an autonomous act, as an act of willful intention. Within this space, the examination of form becomes a question of control in relation to autonomous geometrical forms. As an extension of this idea, the student research focuses on the accumulation of mutations as it pertains to degrees of manipulation. The accumulation of mutation can therefore be interpreted as having latent affective potential.

If, traditionally, design necessitates an expertise in form and proportion, then strategies of mutation are an evolution of that expertise — it cannot escape tradition. Formal mutations are dynamic topologies that preserve their properties while under continuous deformation. They are malleable and in metamorphosis. The structuring of dynamic topologies, to a large degree, pertains, then, to the highest control of those formal manipulations. These techniques of control proliferate a complex taxonomy of structural systems, not as serial iterations, but as groups of familiar mutations. These taxonomies are families of synthetic organisms, composed of indivisible cells whose interaction contaminates the overall system. Where traditional architecture determined the degree of beauty a project achieved through form and proportion, these topologies explore the possibility whereby an excess of form and proportion can achieve the grotesque or horrific. Rooting this topological design paradigm within the confines of architecture's aim for proportion and beauty allows new kinds of structural organizations to produce the grotesque through an excess of necessary variation.

Architectural species is not about biomimicry, nor the insertion of biology into, and onto, architecture. It is, rather, the transference of multiple physiological scales into a system of intelligence. The mutation of cellular logic, at multiple scales, creates a behavioral feedback between form generation and the studio program. The studio used the program of a house as a tool to study the shift toward a paradigm of Species as opposed to the ubiquitous platform of Types. If Types are traditionally viewed as categories of standardization and symbolic expressions of form, then Species are malleable entities that are in constant metamorphosis; adaptation and mutation are the main properties of Species.

Foucault's history of medicine is simultaneously a history of vision that describes a system for both organizing and deforming the body. The body becomes an assemblage layered through time, each historical strata containing its own methodology for organizing and viewing the body. Within the modern regime of medical surveillance, the species becomes an animated corpse, explicated by viewing the body through MRIs and technological dissections. The body is seen as an assemblage of organs into which diagnoses are invested and installed. The inside becomes the outside, or, more precisely, the inside becomes an interior structural condition that stands in relation to another exterior structural condition. The space between these two conditions is an epidermal membrane — a skin — selectively mediating what might pass through.

The design task was deceptively straightforward: House. Critical to the discussion of interiority and structure is the conditional understanding of the irreducible "unit" that comprises architecture. Investigations into what is irreducible in architectural paradigms of structure allowed the studio research to focus on the topic of organization and matter.

The work during the semester evolved into figuring out ideas of contamination that fall outside computational techniques. The house as a topic reshapes the focus on the notion of ritual and the possibility of rituals to be a code for formal transformation. The house is the home of the routine; morning routines, before-bed routines, along with others, often form a daily code of existence. Through robotic repetition, these routines become rituals, and that repetition is what drives rituals to the fringe of our cognitive capacity, becoming codes that one always follows. Most take these routines, these daily rituals, as deterministic matters of fact, but within the studio these codes became generative points to subvert the context of ritual, and therefore house. There is always a question of desire that drives these formal codes within the studio, a desire to alter certain codes as opposed to others as a means to generate affect by confronting the occupant. A close reading of these desires reveals a latent romanticism of in-between lines in the research that acts as an automatic mode of part-to-whole. Part-to-whole as "formalism," which has to do with certain notions of excess and exuberance, is a certain cinematic formalism that allows the possibility of enhancing the "grotesque" as an alternative means to beauty. It could be argued that the work the students produced ended up being more about the driving techniques rather than the desire to subvert rituals, but technique gets one only so far. The studio was also influenced by the notion of aesthetics and how form relates to aesthetics. There are always certain elements that are permanent and those that do not change. At the same time, it is more about looking outside the discipline of architecture for the possibility for mutation and contamination.

To an extent, the studio's focus on the house was an exercise in manipulation and mutations of precedents.

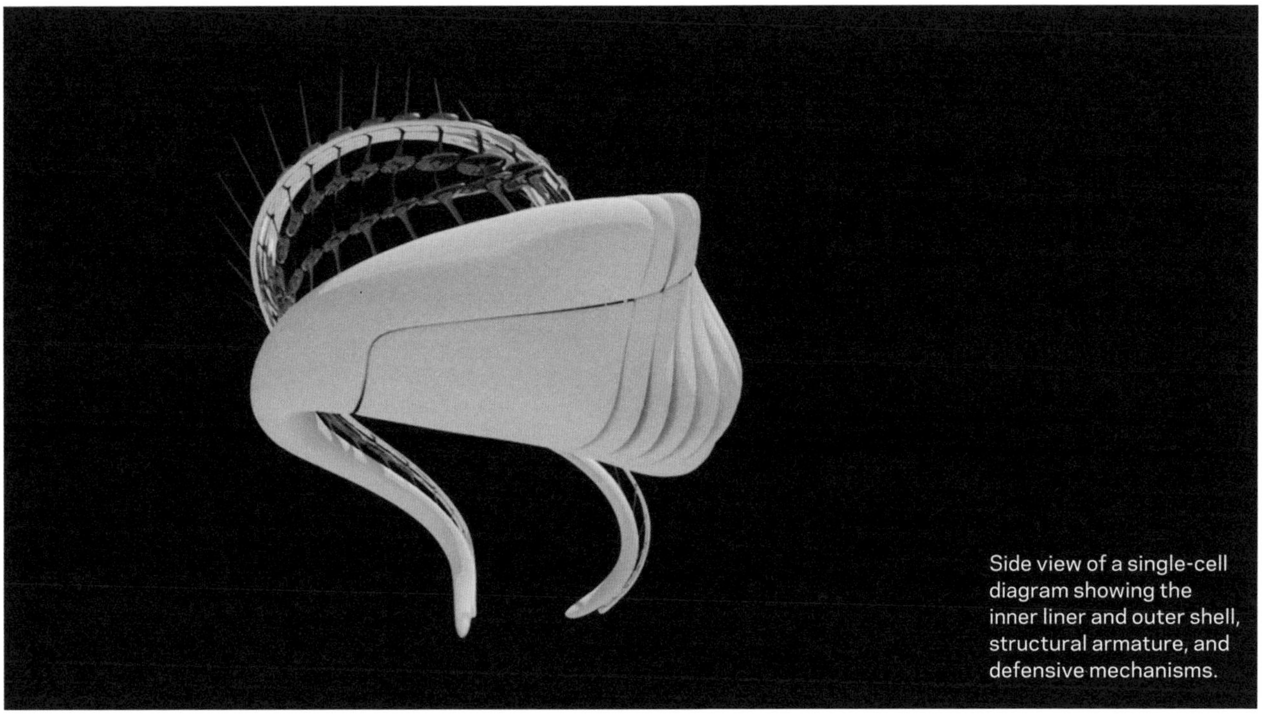

Side view of a single-cell diagram showing the inner liner and outer shell, structural armature, and defensive mechanisms.

What I realized in working through the problem of "the house" is that this was the first time I was being ambivalent about precedent — too many precedents can become paralyzing. To be very clear, I am absolutely convinced that architecture is incapable of producing anything new. At best, architecture can be innovative and produce innovation, but, as a discipline, it can never break from its past or from its memories. Part of looking at history and precedent is not that you don't recognize the past, but, rather, that you have an aggressive attitude to break with it. While it is literally impossible to make a completely clean break with the history of architecture, the idea or expectation that you can challenge history is really important.

I think architecture is a discipline in which you cannot escape history; one has to understand architecture's past. The importance of this is probably true of any discipline, but it is certainly evident in architecture. More often than not, you realize that the work and research being done has similarities with what was produced before. It is always better to have history and precedent in your repertoire than not. At the same time, when you overplay that similarity you risk revisiting some of the nightmares of Post-Modernism. Architects are always revising their own "traditions," revisiting a disciplinary past while moving forward. My sense is that architecture is like a game: you have to keep moving the finish line all the time. I'm all for excess and extremes, so I think it's good to go to an extreme and say, "Forget history or forget contemporary technology. Now, let's look into this particular thing." Forgetting, as an act of suspending what one knows, becomes a way of remembering. In this way, the work within the studio developed into a pendulum between blacks and whites, or a series of polemics, with no attempt to synthesize an androgynous middle, gray ground. Rather than a balance between precedent and innovation, the student work found a third ground beyond mediation, beyond polemics and parameters, that initiates the investigations.

Along these lines, the work produced by the students was provocative, dealing with the banality of "houseness" while trying to define "species" as a way of replacing typology. The projects are self-contained micro-worlds that are trying to redefine new behaviors. For many, the methodology of these projects is like an autopsy process: you are doing it until you're dead, and you might not know what to do with it along the way. The moment it is done, you produce the autopsy; figure out what you can and move on to the next one. It is not that what was done is useless, but, to an extent, it needs to become useless. The projects are much more interested in how than what — that is, in how a project evolves to a developed thing instead of what the thing is. The embryo that evolves into a human is never able to tell the whole story, but its autopsy can tell a life story. It is really

The spatial organization of the interior was inspired by images of parasitic wasps infesting figs, where they gather to lay and hatch eggs.

important to not fall in love with initial ideas; students need to keep moving and changing without any sense of nostalgia.

No matter the fascination with current technology, the question of the house is critical because architecture is, and should remain, an existential problem. It has to remain a humanist problem, and it always needs to reclaim this position as a kind of artistic problem. The good architects are beginning to understand that a project cannot be about only certain things — it has to move beyond current fascinations. The final stage of the studio engaged site and behavioral conditions. At this stage, students had already visited Los Angeles, and each had a collection of images from case studies and site details to inform the final transformation of their designs.

Living in an era of images and effects, we may easily confuse fiction with reality. Fiction is a type of reality. The contemporary explosion of imagery cannot be more exposed than within the artificiality of the Los Angeles landscape. Cinematography, car culture, pollution, and plastic surgery make Los Angeles the quintessential image city — not a postcard city, just an image — and, as such, it epitomizes contemporary culture. Image is the digital currency of contemporary culture, easily transmitted and malleable to any end. Los Angeles' context is a landscape of fictions, an amalgamation of romanticized images that mutates the idea of what a house is.

A studio in which all the research deals with the problem of the "House" self-generates its own context; it creates a sense of familiarity. While the architectural forms may be excessive, they are a family because of this context. In this sense, popular culture is useful to mutate the familiar into something more sophisticated. In a studio driven by the desire for the grotesque, the horrific, and the weird, the familiar makes these qualities worse. Nothing is more horrific than the familiar thing; nothing is more grotesque than the familiar thing.

Studio
Work

01 SPECIES

As the title might suggest, categorical groupings of student projects is a slight misnomer. While categorical distinction is operative from the outside and as a beginning, the evolution of projects relied upon an ability to fluctuate between polemics. If categorical polemics are black and white, the students projects aimed for a third ground, one that is beyond the androgyny of a middle gray. Species do not mediate by compromise; rather, they alter and subvert into something entirely different. As a family, all the studio projects explored the paradigm shift of Species versus Type, yet these particular projects confronted the question of occupation more directly. These projects are Species because they necessitate a different model for occupation — that is, architecture as a device that must be overcome to be occupied.

LIAM LOWRY

EXPLORING PLASTICITY

This studio used the program of the house to study the shift toward a paradigm of Species as opposed to the ubiquitous platform of Types. If types are traditionally viewed as categories of standardization and symbolic expressions of form, then Species are malleable entities that are in constant metamorphosis; that is, adaptation and mutation are the main characteristics of Species. To address this topic, I developed a three-part cell comprising a structure, a skin, and a deformer. The cells were imbued with a growth and aggregation intelligence that made the project more than a singular work of architecture, but rather a systematic intelligence capable of mutation.

01.01 Perspective showing vegetative infiltration.

01.02 Plaster-print sectional model showing detail of mutative interaction.

01.03 Plaster-print sectional model showing parallel interaction with the ground plane.

01 01

01 02

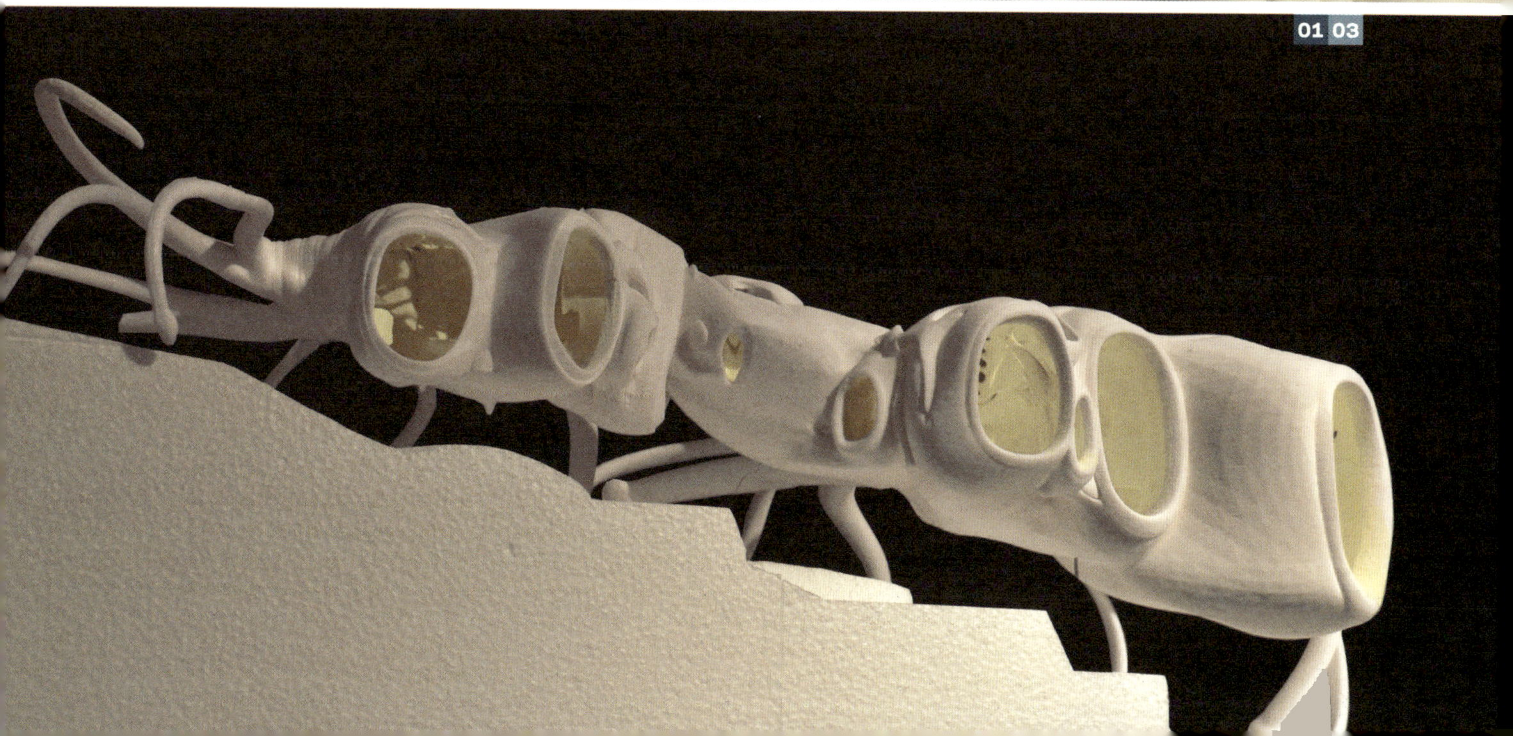
01 03

01 04

01 05

01 06

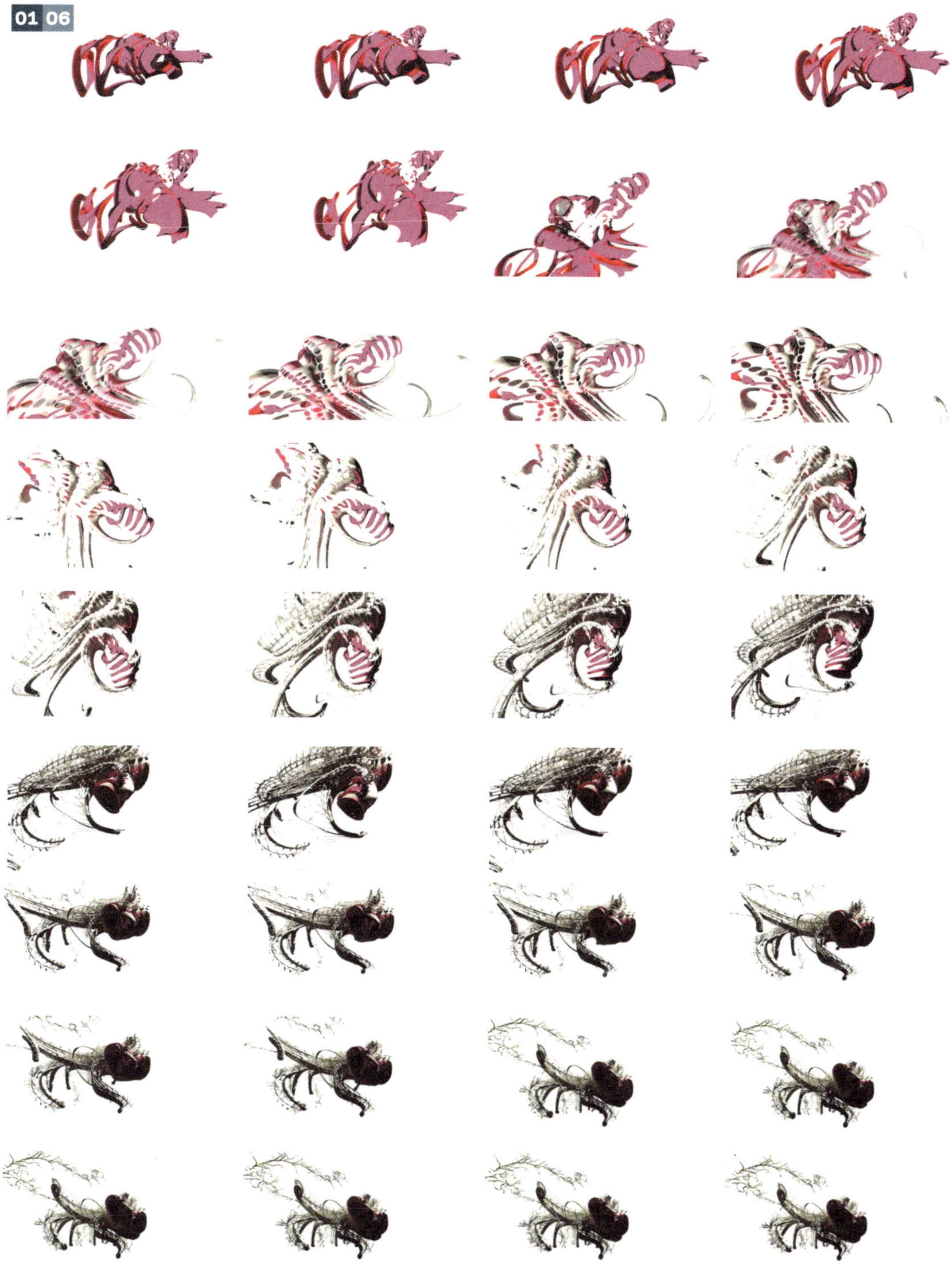

01.04 Film still.

01.05 Oblique scan of the aftermath and division showing spatial entropy.

01.06 Film stills: Mutative interaction.

01 07

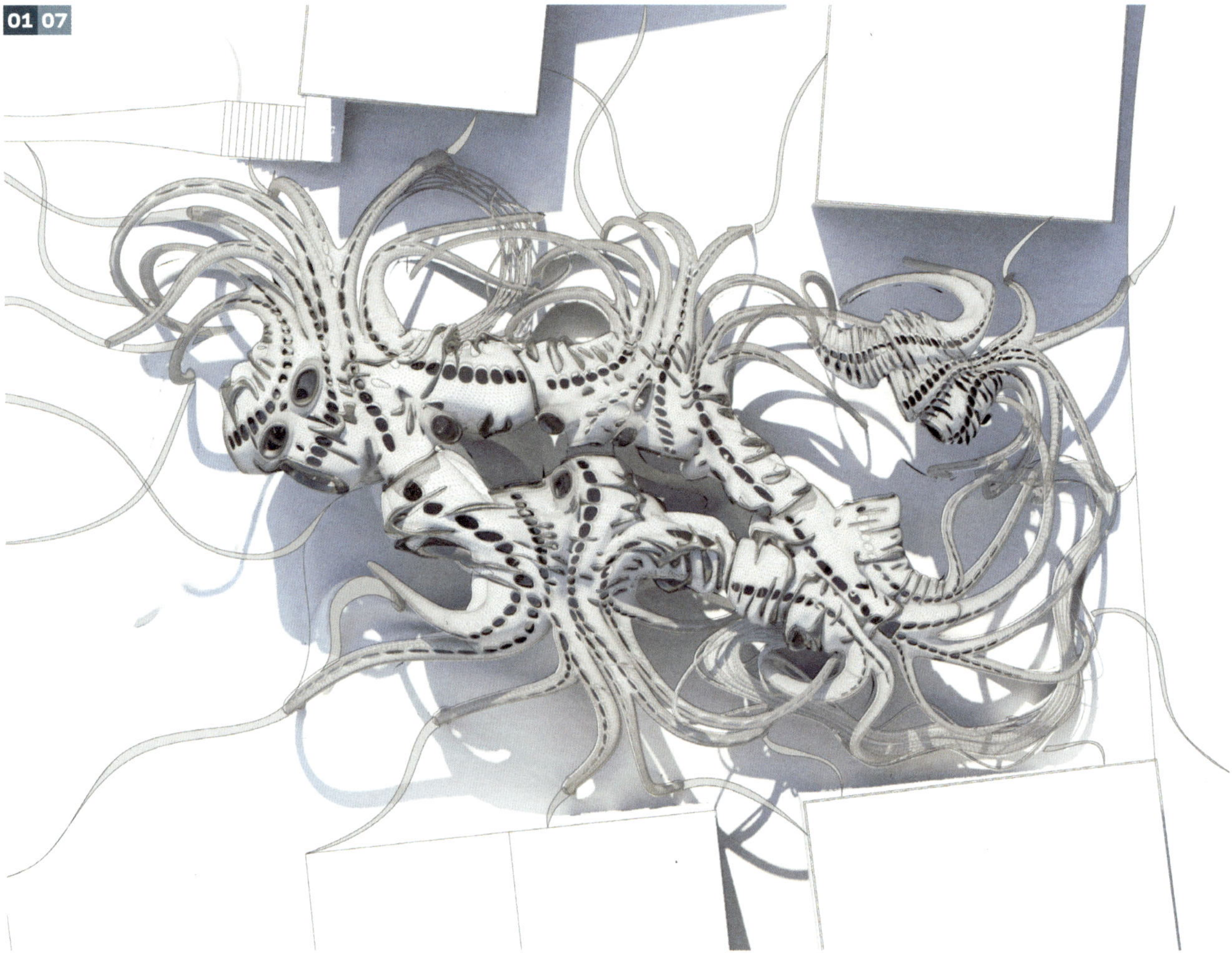

01 08

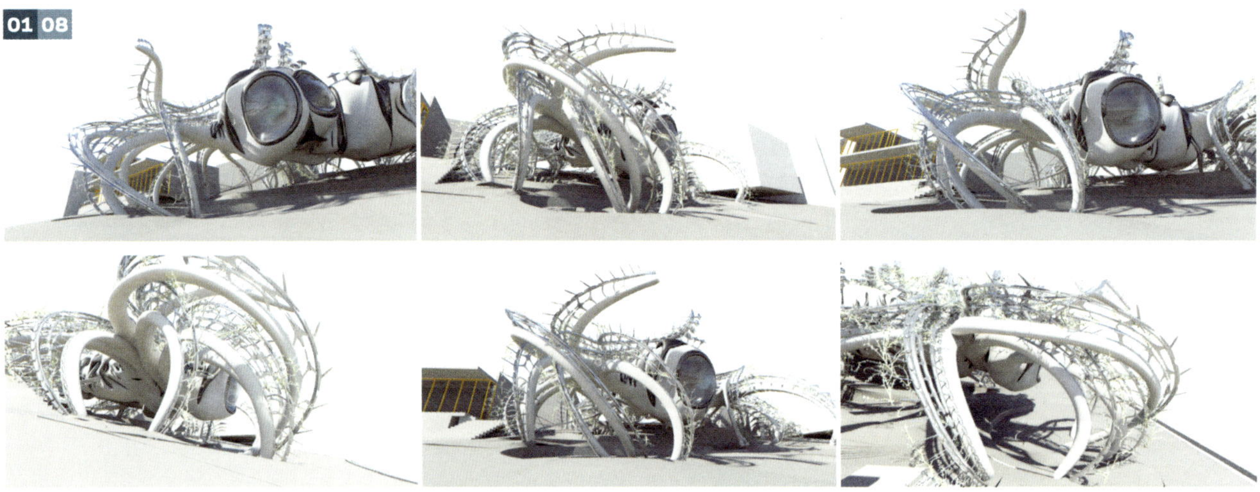

01.07 The spread: Site plan with ground-plane interactions.

01.08 Film stills: Entry sequence with vegetative infiltration.

02.01 Despite an earth-quake, the house and its garden continue to thrive.

ANDREW SMITH-RASMUSSEN

THE HYPERNATURAL HOUSE

Los Angeles. Silverlake. A site that oozes chic Modernism. A conflation of utopian dreams and consumer myopia paints a hazy patina of nostalgia, courtesy of *Dwell* magazine. It is hard to imagine a site less suited to excessive formal and spatial explorations. However, are there trends in the DNA of Los Angeles that can be spliced, manipulated, mutated, or even turned against the city itself?

So-called California High Modernism — Neutra, the Eamses, Koenig, Killingsworth et al. — is typified by privileging the vista, the view across the city and hills. Large expanses of glass and an abundance of sliding doors enable the clichéd "blurring of inside and outside." By the time Modernism landed in Los Angeles, it had lost its socialist agenda and replaced it with a love for lounges, pools, and million-dollar views. Progressive form-making and bourgeois culture became synonymous in California High Modernism. Rather than diffusing the dwelling into society, High Modernism in the Golden State diffused the dwelling into the environment.

The Hypernatural House explores the logic of environmental diffusion beyond the vista-through-window trope. Through this logic, the house invents a new relationship with "the environment" and what the house or the environment could signify today. The first step destroys the house as an object and as a coherent collection

02 02

of parts. In fact, the house is ripped apart and scattered across the site. Sac-like envelopes tumble down the sloped site, coming to rest as misshapen globs of program. In lieu of a corridor, a skeletal catwalk connects the pneumatic sacs. Unlike the hallway, which has a maximum level of privacy and enclosure, the catwalk is minimally enclosed and becomes the baseline armature for enclosure. Covered in lush vegetation, this armature becomes the minimum level of privacy in the house. Like most houses in Los Angeles, the vegetation is as much a part of the house as anything else, and it helps mediate privacy and access. Going one step further, the Hypernatural House's garden is programmed in sync with the house: vegetables grow by the kitchen, fragrant flowers grow by the living sac, aphrodisiacs grow around the master bedroom, and so on. Finally, the armature is ground to a mirror finish, diffusing the house entirely into the environment. As if gazing through warped Claude glass, the curving, convex delirium explodes the space of the house, collapsing the view onto itself, the environment, and the neighborhood. Perception of form is overwhelmed by an endless recursion of the Droste effect. A walk down the corridor sets off infinite micro animations that cascade through the house, erasing origins and boundaries. One cannot tell where the house begins or ends. The construction of the house is its environment, yet the environment is a construct.

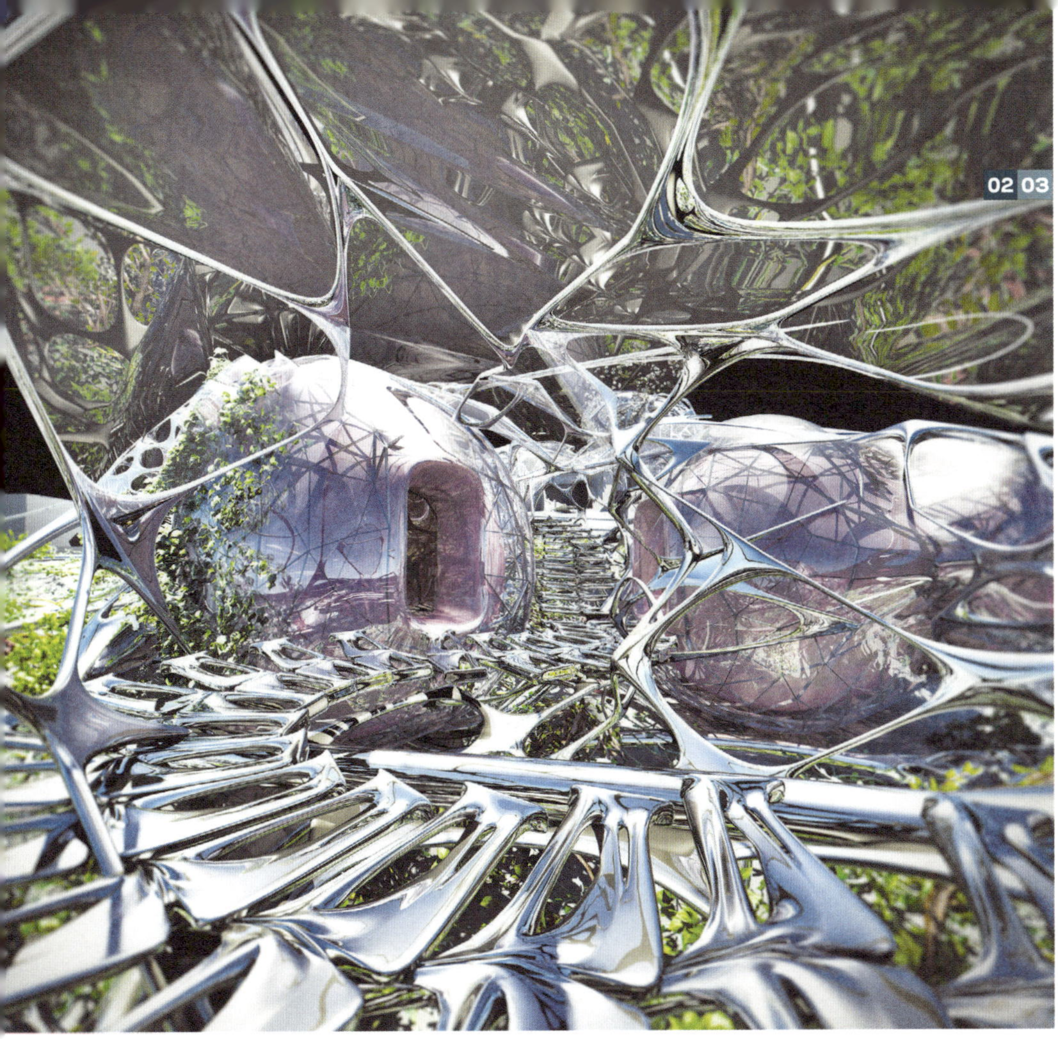

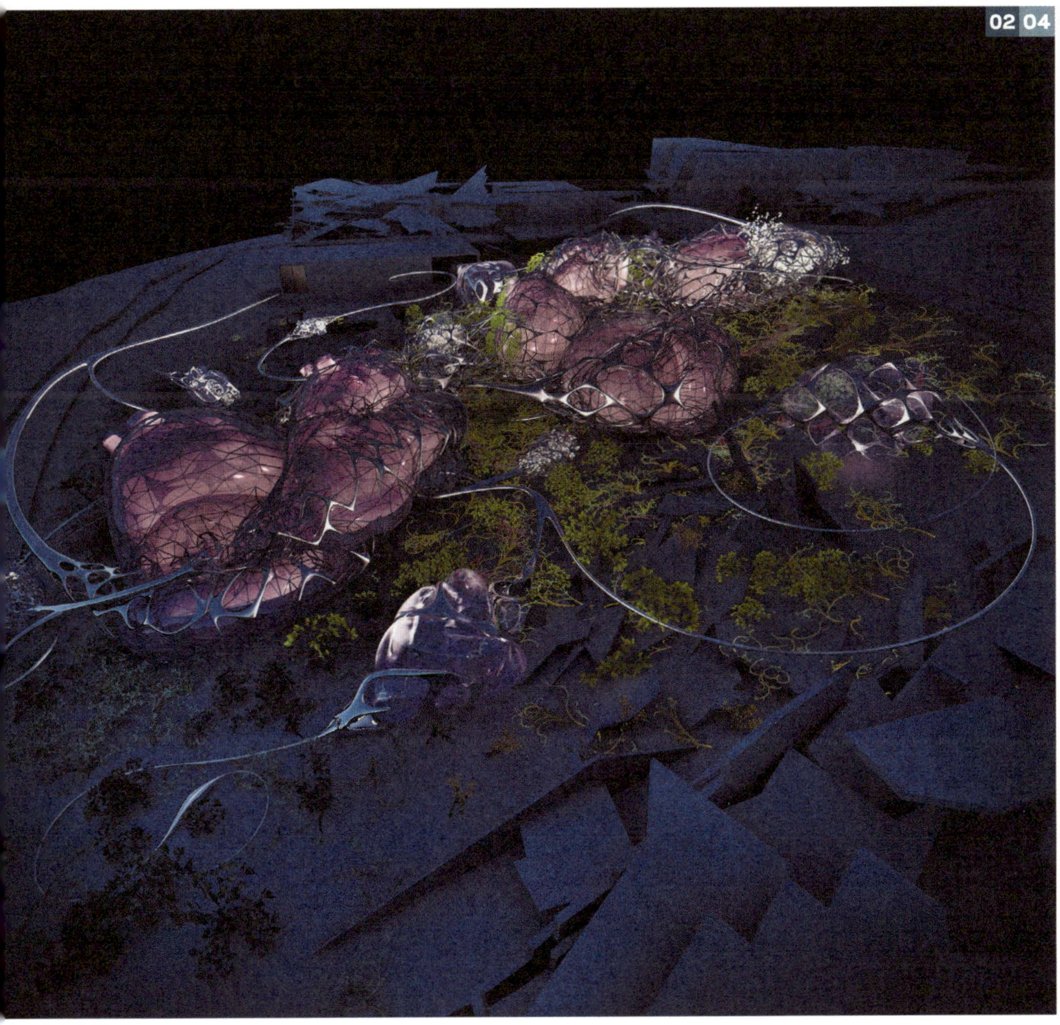

02.02 Unlike its extroverted Modernist neighbors, the new house seeks to cultivate a dynamic private interior through convolution, reflection, and vegetation.

02.03 Moving through the central corridor, one is on view to the neighbors. An abundance of twisted, reflective surfaces camouflages the central corridor.

02.04 At night, the translucent pink skin of the pneumatic program volumes become internal screens, which resemble glowing lanterns, onto which the inside is projected.

03 01

HOEY YIP

(JUST) A HOUSE IN L.A.

A grotesque house in Silver Lake, Los Angeles, the project mutates as it evolves, and, following each mutation, increases in perversity. The project begins with a set of original spherical masses that hold unique functional spaces. These spheres are violently stitched together with spiked thorn cables, which also serve as the structural armature of the house. The action is not unlike how humans were stitched end to end to form one continuous system, in Tom Six's horror film *The Human Centipede*. This system of volumes, which are kept together through tension, can be placed anywhere. The resulting form is a set of tortured volumes, with the skin torn apart through tension, creating creases and apertures. The house evolves and mutates under duress in order to address architectural issues such as habitable space, entry, aperture, a divorce between the occupants, and an earthquake. From the beginning, the building is a living organism, a biological machine.

The spatial organization of the interior takes inspiration from images of parasitic wasps infesting figs, which is where wasps gather to lay and hatch their eggs. The figs, like the spherical volumes, provide all the necessary conditions for

03.01 The products of nanotechnology will be soft, responsive, wet, and smart; they will be grown, grafted, and bred. The pink film that covers the exterior is a layer of smart bacteria, capable of learning and adjusting and constantly evolving to accommodate the needs of the inhabitants.

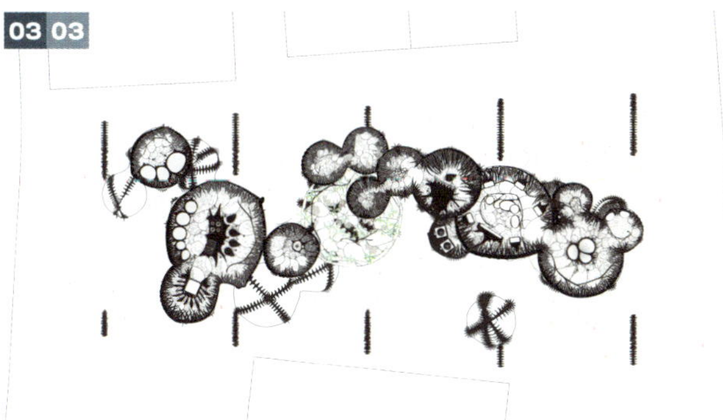

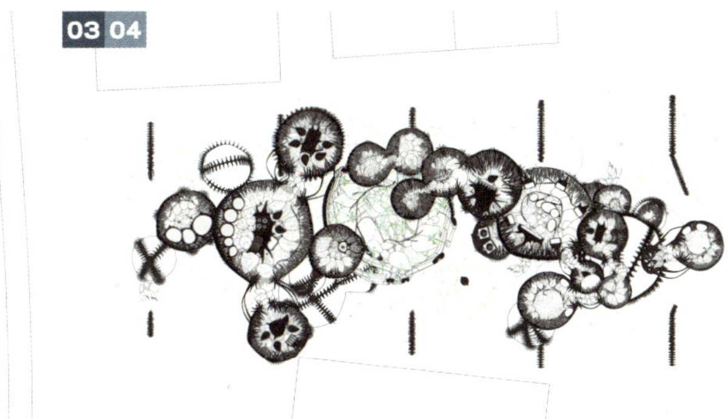

habitation. The wasps feed from the flesh, infesting the fruit with their colonization while preserving the structural integrity of the shell. This type of infestation is in dialogue with the subject-object relationship that Bruno Latour discusses in his essay "Factures/fractures," in which he uses the example of Mafalda regarding her father's act of smoking a cigarette while also observing the cigarette as smoking her father. Is the house being inhabited, or is the inhabitant merely an organism that exists within the living house? The interior of the house evolves in an array of soft spikes, or thumps, which act as receptacles for various prosthetics that can be attached and replaced, similar to the way tools are attached to amputated limbs in films such as Robert Rodriguez's *Planet Terror* or Noburu Iguchi's *The Machine Girl*. The furniture, such as the piano, is mechanically attached to the spike receptacles and awaits human interaction. A new creature has been created.

The project in its current state is at a balance between living and inanimate objects. It is no longer a world created by man, but a world in which man either co-exists with the architecture or is enslaved by it.

03.02 The building becomes a network of bacteria, a wet computer that is in a direct relationship between building and environment. An organic machine, it is constantly sensing and adjusting.

03.03 Floor plan of the original house.

03.04 First mutation floor plan of house after the divorce scenario.

03 05

03 06

03 07

03.05 This type of infestation is in dialogue with the subject-object relationship exemplified in Latour's essay "Factures/fractures," in which Mafalda observes her father smoking a cigarette and the cigarette smoking her father.

03.06 The spatial organization of the interior was inspired by images of parasitic wasps infesting figs, where the wasps gather to lay and hatch eggs.

03.07 Close-up view of sectional model.

02 PRIMITIVES

"Primitives" are horrifically familiar building blocks, irreducible geometric units that form the DNA of potentially excessive mutations. Seemingly benign in nature, geometric primitives include spheres, boxes, and other platonic solids one might recall from early childhood development devices such as Froebel blocks. The cognition of a primitive and its mutated other creates a tension in perception, a dubiously indeterminate system that confronts the viewer. Perceiving this system's borders, if such things exist, reveals an architecture precariously caught between the familiar and its own delirious nightmare. Placing square pegs in round holes is more than a potential strategy; it is the baseline for a type of behavioral logic that contaminates an entire system.

YANG GUANG

ORPHEUS RESIDENCE

This project takes on the Greek myth of Orpheus and Eurydice as a narrative to comprehend the actions of a domestic dwelling as a method to develop architecture. In this modern sequel, Orpheus, now in his mid-forties, is a harpist with the Los Angeles Philharmonic. His first wife, Eurydice, died twenty years ago, not long after their marriage, and left him with a drug-addicted son. Orpheus then married Jane, with whom he has a nine-year-old daughter. The domestic tension is both metaphor and a cause for mutation in the structural elements and the enclosure components. This relationship is alternately twisted, exaggerated, neutralized, hidden, and exposed by the domestic undercurrent of this complex modern family.

The rigid methodology of the initial organization, laid out in a grid of columns, echoes Richard Neutra's structures to the north of the site. However, a series of circles are introduced to intentionally complicate and blur the relationship between structure and enclosure. Each room is a mutation of an enclosure cell, while the columns are variations on Neutra's original structure. Through the process of mutation, the architecture of this single-family home becomes intertwined with the identities of the adjacent four residents. Rooms are kept separate and distinct from each other. The form of each enclosure is influenced by the

structure as well as by the adjacent enclosures. Rooms, circulation, landscape, and views are organized, yet also violated, by the columns and circles.

The project is a snap shot into the life of Orpheus's family. The architecture continually evolves and mutates with the ongoing relationships between the family members.

01 03

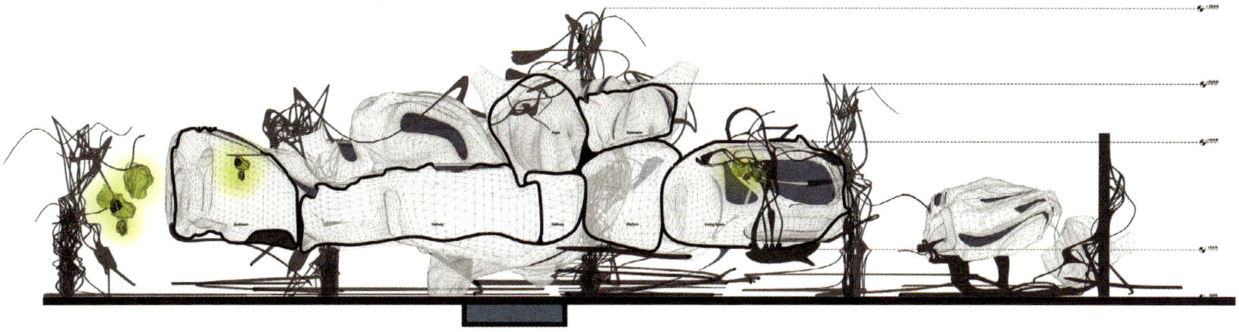

01 04

01 05

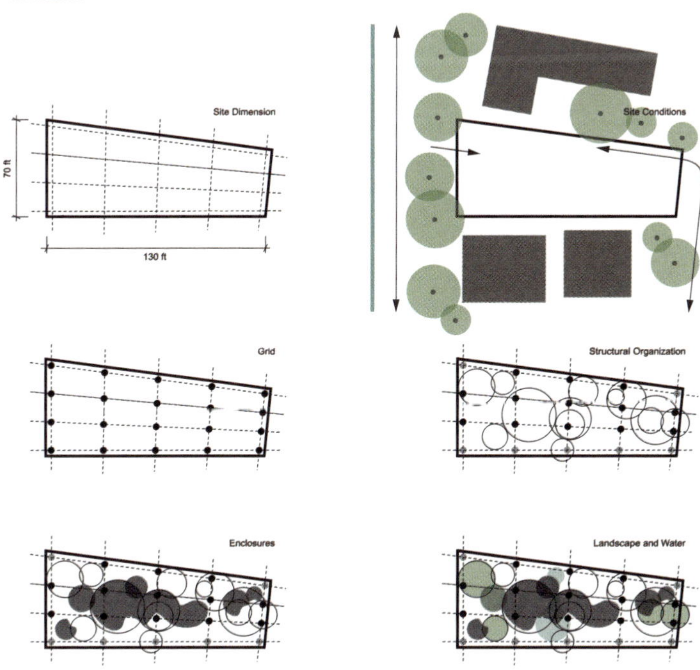

01.01 Jane and her daughter playing at the pool.

01.02 Orpheus in the dining room.

01.03 Longitudinal section.

01.04 The first-floor plan.

01.05 Site strategy.

EMER O'DALY

ORNAMENT AND THE FRACTAL DIMENSION

In *The Fractal Geometry of Nature*, Benoit Mandelbrot writes that, "in the context of architecture, a Mies van der Rohe building is a scale-bound throwback to Euclid, while a high-period Beaux Arts building is rich in fractal aspects." Mandelbrot identifies both the Palais Garnier and the Eiffel Tower as examples of scaling objects, that is, architecture with fractal qualities. For much of the twentieth century, architecture has been dominated by the Modernist style, which is characterized by simple, primary shapes devoid of ornament or extraneous detail, in contrast with the richly ornamented buildings of previous periods. If one visually compares Modern architecture with what came before, one of the most striking differences lies in the profiles, or edges, of these architectural styles. The outline of Modern architecture is flat, sharp, and smooth, while the edges and surfaces of Classical architecture have a more meandering or rough appearance. This striking visual difference is at the scale of ornament and its applications.

The most popular understanding of fractal geometry is that fractals are self-similar; however, they may also be described as the field of mathematics that describes the geometry of the edges of natural forms. Fractal geometry describes the mathematics of mediation in nature through edges, while, in pre-Modern architecture, ornament mediates the edges of forms.

In describing fractal shapes, Mandelbrot uses the words *grainy, hydra-like, in between, pimply, pocky, ramified, seaweedy, strange, tangled, tortuous, wiggly, wispy, wrinkled.* Similarly, in architecture, these characteristics can also be used to describe the undulating surfaces and edges of much traditional ornamented architecture. Man-made forms with crinkled profiles and staggered edges represent the influence of fractal geometry. Additionally, this fractal aspect usually

02.01 Courtyard view: A play of ornament culminates in the central courtyard and stairs.

02.02 Column capital inspired by Hector Guimard and Louis Sullivan.

becomes evident at the scale of ornament. When architects say that ornament "imports" or "super-adds" a new element into a building, along with the cultural significance and symbolic meaning it imbues, it also brings, quite literally, a new dimension. Ornamentation gives the edges of the form a fractal dimension.

With the advent of non-standard fabrication processes and digital tools in architecture, surfaces are once again being patterned, perforated, contoured, folded, textured, tessellated, and, essentially, ornamented in an infinite variety of ways. The studio research developed a contemporary language of ornament with the aim of re-introducing the seaweedy, strange, tangled, tortuous, wiggly, wispy, and wrinkled surfaces back into the architectural lexicon. By limiting the large scale of the spaces to primitive Euclidean geometries, a counterpoint is provided to the complex surfaces and shapes at smaller scales.

This language of ornament draws on Classical column design and the work of Louis Sullivan as well as the whiplash curves of Victor Horta and Hector Guimard. The development of the forms began with a single cell that was multiplied and transformed using various symmetry operations. Single cells became families of cells, each mutated in some way from the original, but each tracing their lineage back to the original. In this way, the motifs of ornament were evolved using a limited set of tools and operations. These motifs were then used to bind together the Euclidean forms. The sinuous surfaces proliferate rhythmically at the boundaries and edges of the spaces. The ornament culminates in the central courtyard, where a staircase unwinds through a canopy of leaf-and-stem motifs.

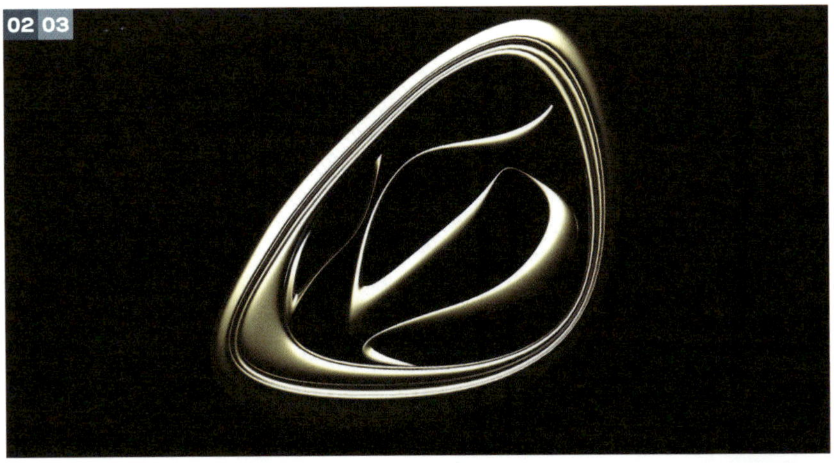

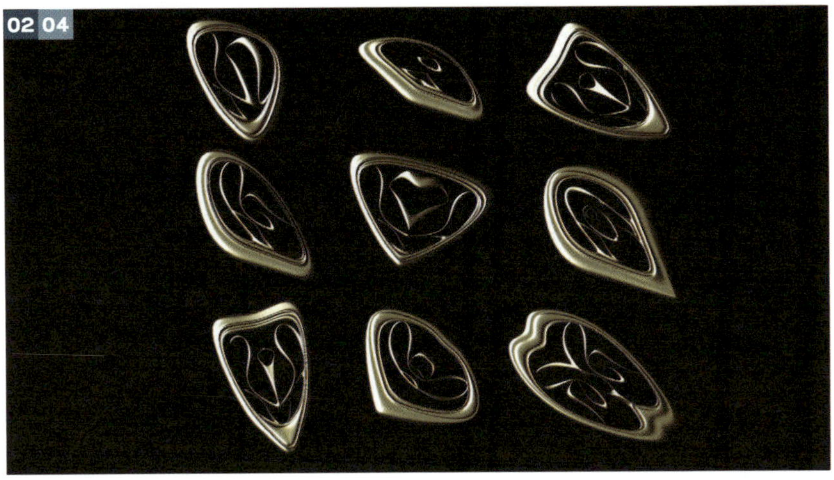

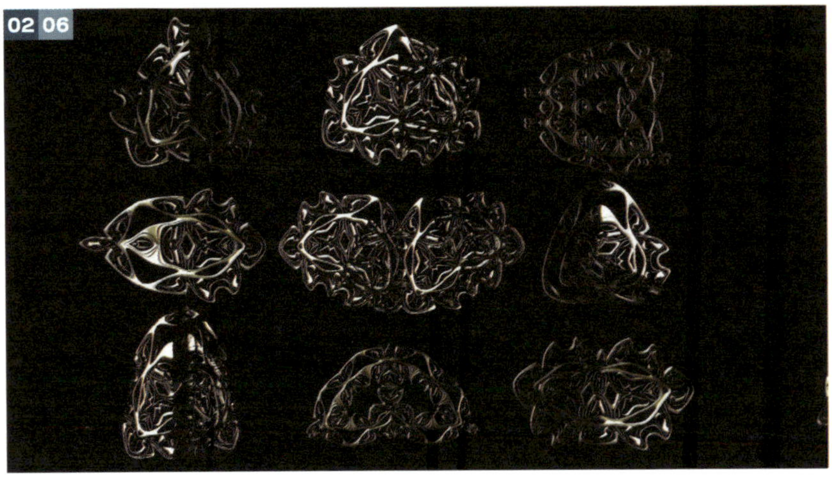

02.03 Basic generative unit.

02.04 Various geometric figures derived from basic generative unit.

02.05 Complex generative unit.

02.06 Various volumetric geometric figures derived from basic generative unit.

JIN KIM

PROTECTIVE SKIN

James was living in a nested concrete shell. Emily was living under a net-like tent. When Emily moved in, she brought her net to cover herself, and James had to accept it to welcome his lover. James had the idea to install Emily's net onto his shell: break the shells and fix them in-between. They bought red tables to step on or lie down upon. For their kids, they built a small pavilion that looks like the house itself. There was an earthquake in the city, and the house collapsed. They blamed each other and hated each other, so they clogged the path to block each other from escaping.

The first step in the design process was to develop architectural elements that represent structure and skin. The next step was to combine them in such a way that these elements would exemplify misfit elements. Instead of creating a structure that supports skin or a skin that protects the structure, this project offers a structure and skins that cannot hold or cover anything very well. The way to combine the incompetent elements was to sacrifice one of them in an awkward way. The result of this process is the first evolution of the house. Then, within the house, I started placing the project's third element, the furniture, which is the most practical and systematic element of the three. Following the setup of the studio, the house was mutated through an earthquake and a divorce between the occupants. While experiencing these changes, the two fundamental elements (structure and skin) were broken and torn. The furniture replicated itself to an extreme and enabled the house to function in these radically different conditions.

03.01 Section model cutting through the living room and the husband's area.

03 02

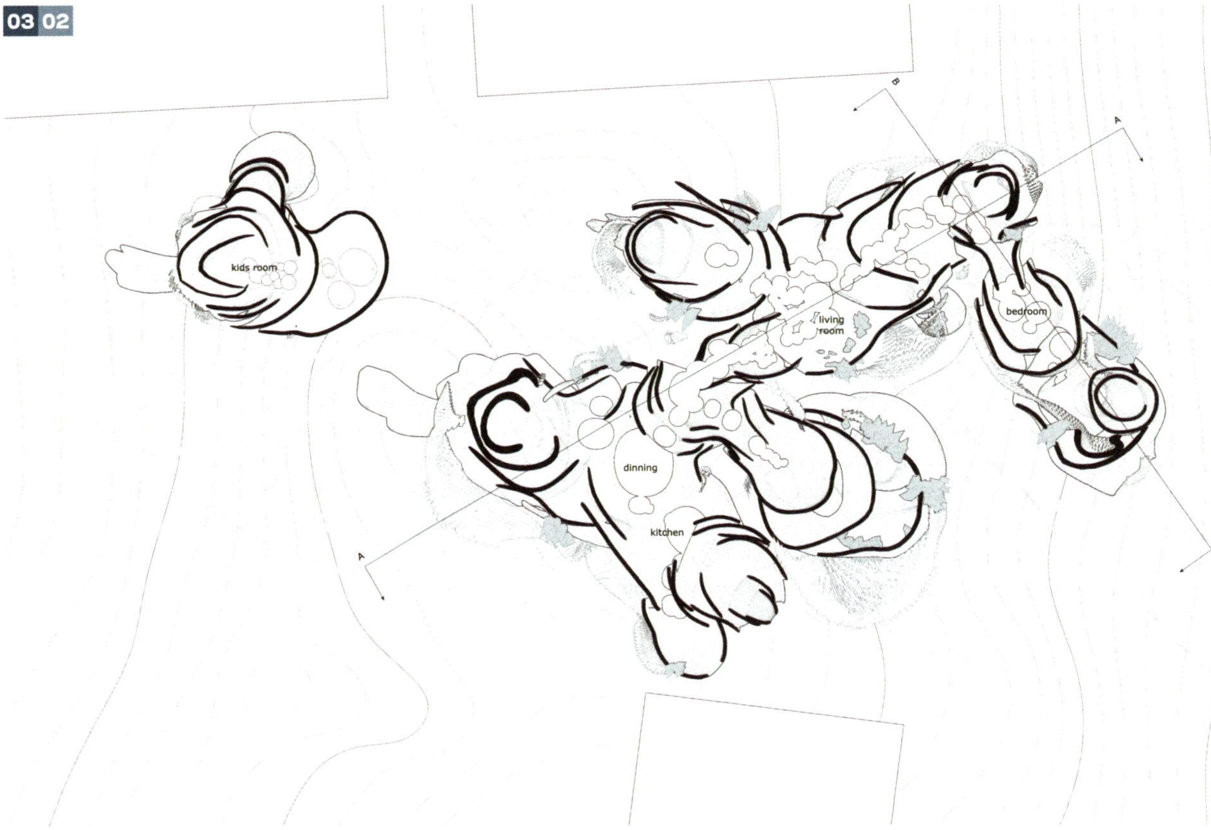

03 03

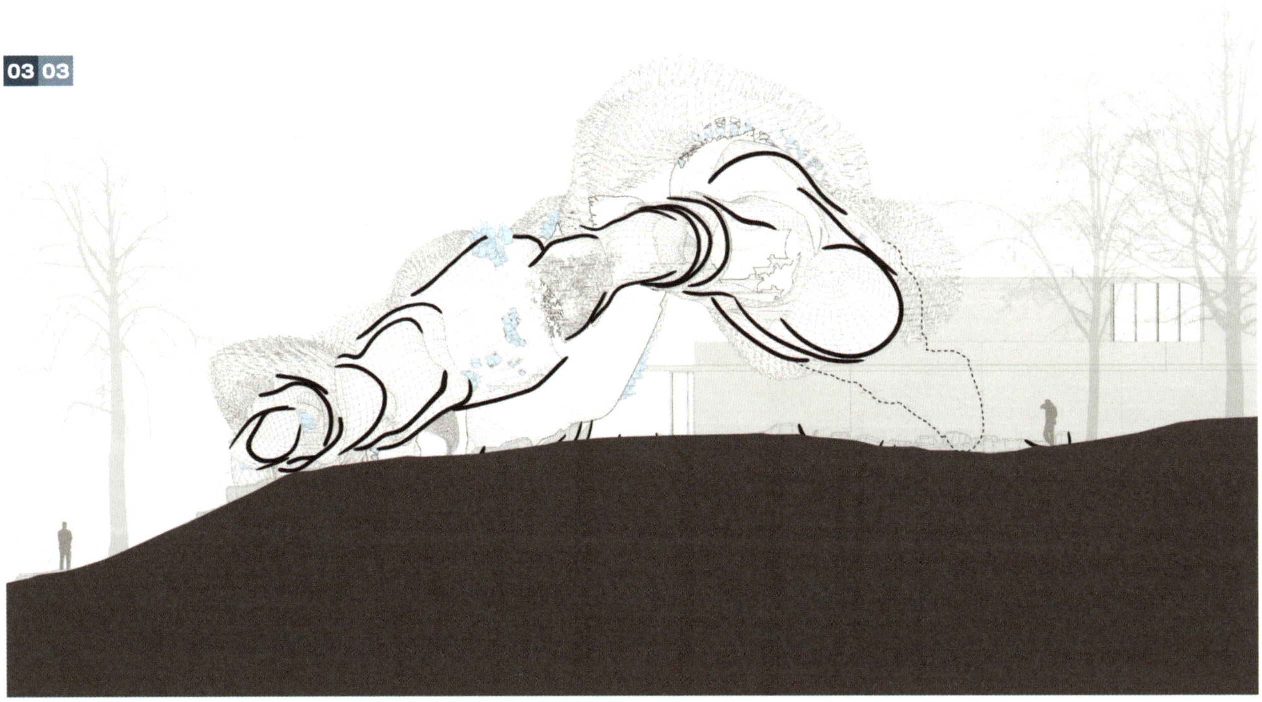

03 04

03 05

03.02 Plan.

03.03 Section.

03.04 Patio space between skin and structure.

03.05 View from the front yard.

03 CELLULAR LOGIC

Cells are animated corpses, diagnosed and installed with behaviors generated from interactions at multiple physiological scales. Cellular logic is one of aggregation and multiplicity, a strategy focused on the interactions among the many. A recursive association between the single and the multiple generates a logic of malleable connections, a taxonomy of mutations generated from potential interactions. Logics of connection feed back into the cells themselves, contaminating a cell as a result of the connection or occasionally spawning an entirely new cell to connect to the existing cell. An autopsy might be able to reveal the origin of a cell. However, its origins never matter in cellular logic; rather, its the effect of ending that determines the potential of this architecture.

KYLE STOVER

A HOUSE IS NOT A HOME

Cuts, scars, and other bodily imprints embody a partial history of one's past. They are marks that reveal an incomplete story. In opposition to the whitewashed subject of modernity, this house embeds tactile narratives into the domestic body as a culmination of the occupants' actions. The house is a product of the actions applied to it, both in its construction as well as in its destruction. Weathered from use and rusticated from repair, this project presents itself as a fragment — a memory of itself. This is not a home for a family concerned with who drew on the walls, but rather who did not.

This project evolves and mutates the house over time while a fiction is played out from within the house. Fictions and half-truths are the formal codes that underwrite each mutation, challenging traditional rituals of occupation. A house is not a home because a home is in stasis; a house is a mutable logic that adapts to needs and desires. In this context, fictions become irreducible formal cells, and the narrative construction logic becomes the formal cellular logic, the fiction of tectonics.

01.01 Still frame: Desire becomes suppressed and starved.

01.02 "Not drawings": Plans and sections often leave space bisected and dissected.

01.03 Model.

01.04 Still frame: On excessive possibilities.

01 01

01 02

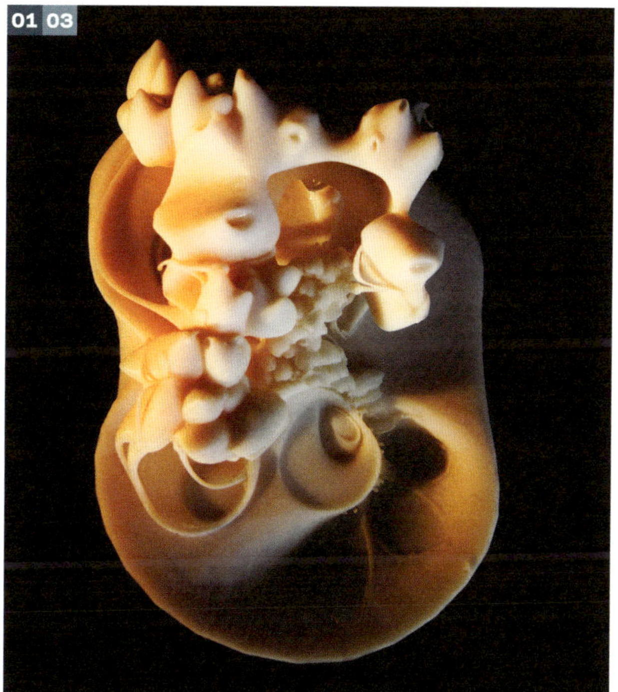
01 03

01 04

01 06

Situated between a series of Richard Neutra houses whose real estate reality undermines the utopic fantasy of their conception, the project opens a context to internal subversion. The story of capitalism's absorption of Neutra's socially liberated dream is well rehearsed, but the story of capitalizing on the excess of such an economy is a new one — possibly even an invented one. Californian capitalism has converted the Los Angeles house into a platform for a modern-day Howard Roark to consume an unlimited vista, a disenfranchised vehicle that distracts from his impotence. To undermine this consumption, this house has nothing to look at, nowhere to go, nothing to offer. Words like "enclosure," "room," or "bedroom" are dubious distinctions with endless annotations that rarely explicate such consequences.

From the beginning, the foster family who occupies this house never belonged; they are a socially disconnected surplus. The need to live off the land creates a series of elevated living cells shrouded in wall-like layers of productive vegetation. These vegetated walls obfuscate all views while heavily filtering light or anything else that may attempt to enter. The living cells and vegetation are surgically wired together with metallic prosthetics, mutilating through an attempt to stabilize. As the foster family grows and contracts, the living cells are continually mutated to accommodate changes in the family dynamic. They are an endless series of spaces, precariously held together by what appears to be a structure — at least from the outset. The house becomes an infinite internal view, an inescapable system — a fiction of the home.

01.06 Partial versions: At some point, one may have considered these as possible futures or possible pasts. Perhaps they came first, but most likely they came last.

PATRICK DELAHOY

CELLULAR ARMATURE

Fundamental to the character of the iconic Los Angeles house is the spatial intersection of intense seclusion with breathtaking vistas. Generally shrouded from a street view with walls and vegetation, these houses award fortunate visitors with sweeping hillside panoramas. In this context, this project proposes a contemporary single-family house for a divorced couple that is sited adjacent to several Neutra case-study houses that overlook the Silver Lake Reservoir.

The house sits a third of the way down the site's slope, occluding its entry from the access street. A spiral stair adjacent to the driveway offers entry to the main lower- and upper-level living spaces. Each ex-spouse occupies his or her own floor and has access to a private terrace. The upper-floor dweller can access a separate garden terrace at ground level via a private spiral stair, while the lower-floor dweller can access an upper-level garden. Private spaces nest but never merge, except for the main garden and lowest terrace, which is also shared.

One aim of the studio was to produce space with variable units, or cells, smaller than room-size but larger than individual bricks or stones. This method of space-making demands a set of rules to regulate similarity and difference as well as a meaningful logic of aggregation. Each cell proposed here is topologically identical — it contains the same number of openings for conduits or connections — but is mutated differently. The cells condense to describe the main volume of the house and its ancillary spaces, such as the garden walls, the garage, and the gazebo.

Steel and glass are the house's primary materials. The bearing armature is steel, which springs from the ground in the form of three overlapping arches to take the vertical load of the glass. Other steel members act as lateral bracing or pipes for water, electrical, and HVAC conduits, which connect to the city grid via the driveway. The glass cells create conditions of privacy in two ways: their twisted geometries bend and reflect light to render illegible anything contained behind them, while, at night, the house is illuminated by tracks of exterior lighting, producing a strong glare from the glass units. This artificial lighting can vary in color and intensity, and programmed patterns can produce an active and engaging spectacle for drivers on Silver Lake Boulevard.

02.01 View from the north: The house accepts and refracts hues from a smoggy sunset over Silver Lake Reservoir.

02 01

02 02

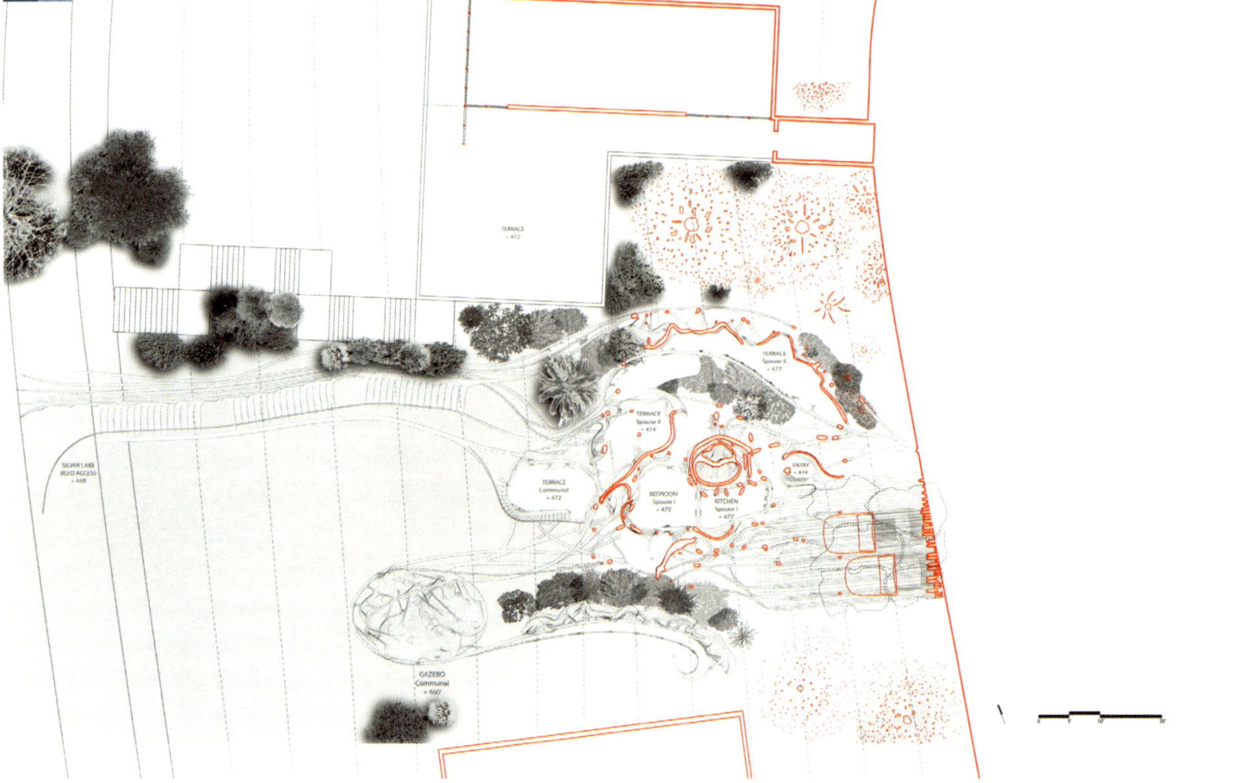

02 03

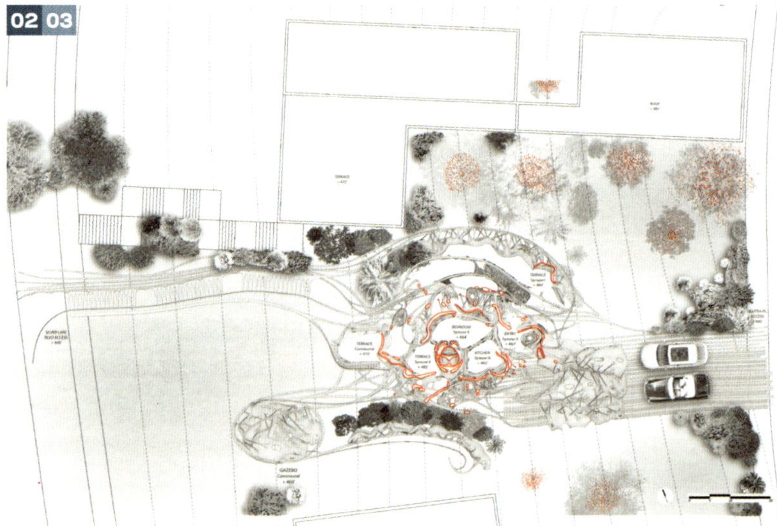

02 04

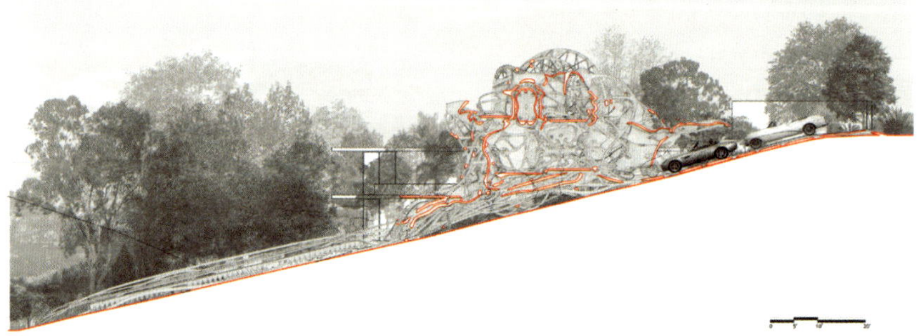

02 05

02 06

02.02 Ground-level plan: A shared entry stair adjoining the driveway gives way to the living floor for one spouse.

02.03 Second-floor plan: The other spouse occupies this floor and a lower-level terrace to the north, accessed via a private spiral staircase.

02.04 Long section: The house perches on the hillside, screened from the street by foliage and splaying downhill toward the lake.

02.05 Perspective from Silver Lake Boulevard: Walking toward the house from below reveals a mass of steel and glass set into the surrounding vegetation.

02.06 Program diagram: Living spaces are nested so that each spouse occupies a living space on one floor and a terrace on another.

GARY KU
HOUSE IN A FIELD OF FIGURES

This project for a California house investigates the use of "loose" spaces, which are formed from a series of curving walls, creating a "house" within a field of gentle volumes.

Typically, classical volumetric space is formed by hard, binary divisions, accessed through binary mechanisms — for example, a door is either open or closed — and a house so divided functions accordingly. This creates a rigid hierarchy among programs. A "loose" space is one formed from soft, variable divisions that gradually increase or decrease in amplitude. In plan, such spaces are formed by a single line curving back upon, but never actually touching, itself. The system of curves serves to loosely define spaces within relatively stronger and weaker "lobe" figures. When combined with several other lines, a field of figures begins to emerge. Volume is created by extruding curves upward and downward to varying degrees and according to programmatic necessity, spatial variety, and a desire for enclosure and shelter versus light and openness.

Activities occur in areas of greater or lesser privacy and varying formal densities. Programs settle within a web of local relationships involving distance, density, and a shifting boundary. The house is animated by warm breezes; flowers and fruit trees rustle at the edges, and sunlight falls within and plays upon a landscape of gently rising and falling curved surfaces. Created for the sunny, arid climate and casual culture of Southern California, the final result is a formal housing typology that is utterly divorced from foreign, formal and tectonic expressions of living.

03 02

03 03

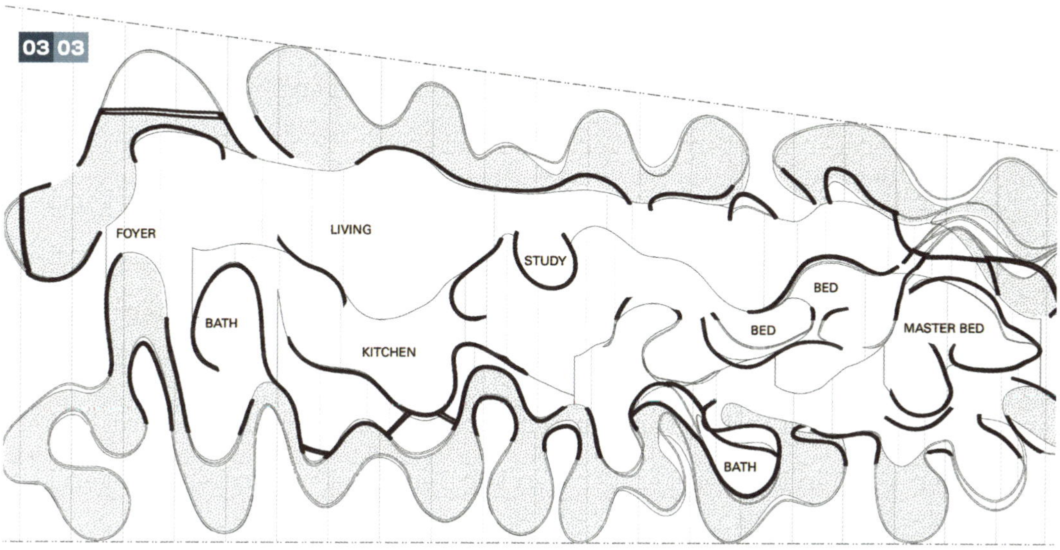

03 04

03.01 View of the master bedroom: The relative privacy of the bedroom is guarded by large, curving walls that leave only a narrow opening for access.

03.02 Final model.

03.03 Plan.

03.04 View from interior hallway toward the living room.

03 05

03 06

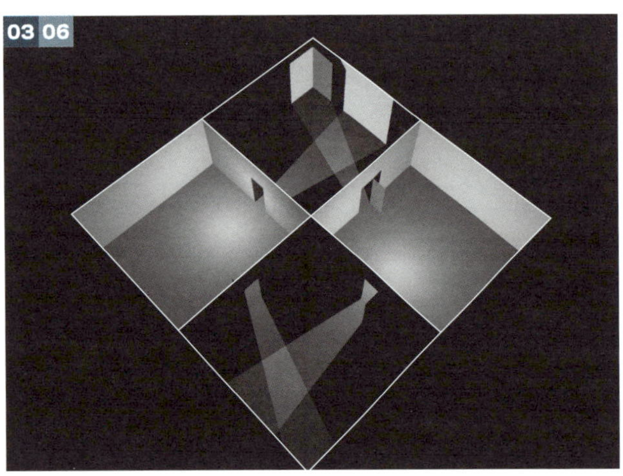

03 07

03.05 House on the site in Silver Lake.

03.06 Rigid space: Typically, classical volumetric space is formed by hard, binary divisions, accessed through binary mechanisms — for example, a door is either open or closed. A house so divided functions accordingly, thus creating a rigid hierarchy among programs.

03.07 Loose space: A "loose" space is one formed by soft, variable divisions. Activities occur in areas of greater or lesser privacy and of more or less formal densities. Programs settle within a web of local relationships, dynamically formed and without explicit boundaries.

03.08 View of the showers and veranda: The showers are surrounded by lush greenery and bathed in natural sunlight.

03.09 View of the study: Small, individual programs are tucked into similarly small, tight "nooks" formed by tight curves.

Image Credits

AOC: 66, 68, 75; Dominik Gigler: 71; Erik Herrmann: 77, 78; Hoey Yip: 128; Lebanese Ministry of Tourism: 19; L.E.FT: 14, 18, 20, 21, 23, 24; Liam Lowry: 127; Maps Geosystems: 22; Nathan Willock: 10; Pietro Savorelli: 13; Xefirotarch/Hernán Díaz Alonso: 118, 120, 121, 122, 123.